Saving Christianity?

MICHAEL YOUSSEF

Saving Christianity

The Danger in Undermining Our Faith— and What You Can Do about It

TYNDALE
MOMENTUM®

The Tyndale nonfiction imprint

Visit Tyndale online at www.tyndale.com.

Visit Tyndale Momentum online at www.tyndalemomentum.com.

TYNDALE, Tyndale's quill logo, *Tyndale Momentum*, and the Tyndale Momentum logo are registered trademarks of Tyndale House Publishers. Tyndale Momentum is the nonfiction imprint of Tyndale House Publishers, Carol Stream, Illinois.

Saving Christianity?: The Danger in Undermining Our Faith—and What You Can Do about It

Designed by Jennifer Phelps

Published in association with Don Gates of the literary agency The Gates Group; www.the-gates-group.com.

For information about special discounts for bulk purchases, please contact Tyndale House Publishers at csresponse@tyndale.com, or call 1-800-323-9400.

Library of Congress Cataloging-in-Publication Data
Names: Youssef, Michael, author.
Title: Saving Christianity? : the danger in undermining our faith - and what you can do about it / Dr. Michael Youssef.
Description: Carol Stream, Illinois : Tyndale House Publishers, 2020. | Includes bibliographical references.
Identifiers: LCCN 2019045140 (print) | LCCN 2019045141 (ebook) | ISBN 9781496441690 (trade paperback) | ISBN 9781496441706 (kindle edition) | ISBN 9781496441713 (epub) | ISBN 9781496441720 (epub)
Subjects: LCSH: Christianity—Essence, genius, nature. | Christianity—Forecasting.
Classification: LCC BT60 .Y68 2020 (print) | LCC BT60 (ebook) | DDC 230—dc23
LC record available at https://lccn.loc.gov/2019045140
LC ebook record available at https://lccn.loc.gov/2019045141

Printed in the United States of America

26   25   24   23   22   21   20
7   6   5   4   3   2   1

Contents

INTRODUCTION Does Christianity Need to Be Saved? *1*

PART ONE The Slide toward Compromise
   1 A Short History of Spiritual Defection *9*
   2 Destroying Christianity by "Saving" It *35*
   3 The Extinction of Truth *61*
   4 The Post-Truth Church in a Post-Christian World *81*
   5 How Biblical Truth Has Shaped History *99*

PART TWO A Christianity without Compromise
   6 I Believe in God the Father *125*
   7 I Believe in Jesus the Son *139*
   8 I Believe in the Holy Spirit *165*

PART THREE Grace and Truth Together
   9 Living Out an Uncompromised Faith *185*

EPILOGUE "That Born Again Thing" *205*
   Notes *211*
   About the Author *223*

Does Christianity Need to Be Saved?

A friend—let's call him Jack—recently told me a story that broke my heart. I'm sure it breaks the heart of Jesus, as well.

"My wife found Christ and was baptized in a nondenominational community church," Jack told me. "She grew up there, and she and I were married in that church by the pastor who founded it. The pastor was a godly man who preached the gospel. He taught the entire Bible, from Genesis to Revelation, as the inspired Word of God.

"I remember sitting in his office with my bride-to-be for our premarital counseling. The most important thing he wanted to know about me was this: Was Jesus my Lord and Savior? Was I a genuine, Bible-believing Christian? Would the Bible have absolute authority over my conduct as a husband and as a Christian?

"Years went by, and that godly minister passed away. The church board called a new minister.

"When the new pastor arrived, he said all the right things and professed to be an evangelical Christian. But over time, his message changed. He told the congregation he was 'evolving' in his faith. He stopped calling the Bible 'the Word of God,' and began calling it 'the book about God' or 'the book that contains God's message.' If you asked him whether the Bible is inspired by God, he'd say, 'Parts of the Bible are so relevant and life-changing that you'd have to call them "inspired by God."' If you asked him whether people needed a Savior, he'd tell you, 'Some people need God, others don't. God isn't offended by those who don't need him.' He once called himself 'an agnostic who loves Jesus.'

"Obviously, this man was not an evangelical Christian. He didn't preach the gospel of salvation by grace through faith in Jesus Christ—the gospel on which the church was founded. As it became clear that this pastor had fallen away from orthodox, biblical faith, some board members tried to oppose him, but others supported him.

"Hundreds of people who had faithfully attended and supported the church began leaving in disillusionment. Over a few years, the church dwindled from a membership of around nine hundred to less than one hundred.

"With so few donors, the congregation could no longer afford to maintain the buildings of that once-thriving church. The pastor and the board sold the church site to a secular business. Today, the tiny congregation still exists under its original name, but without a permanent location. The people meet in various places, wherever they can find a meeting place. Sometimes they meet in a city park or in a senior living center. Of course, there's nothing wrong with a church holding services out in the community, especially as a form of evangelistic outreach. But that's not what this church is doing. It was forced to sell off the physical legacy of its evangelical past because it no longer preaches the gospel of Jesus Christ.

"The original name of that church still exists as words on a website. But the church where my wife and I were married is dead. I looked at the website recently, and it's filled with clichés and slogans: 'We are a progressive Christian community.' 'Love wins.' 'There's more faith in searching than in certainty, in questions than in answers.' 'We're about having a conversation, not indoctrination.'

"This idea they call 'progressive Christianity' has already killed one church. Like a cancer, it's metastasizing and trying to kill all of orthodox, evangelical Christianity. The people in the church where my wife and I were married didn't see it coming. They were blindsided. People need to be warned. They need to know how dangerous these ideas are."

The Threat from the Inside

We live in times of spiritual and moral confusion. So-called progressive Christianity is infiltrating and seducing the evangelical church—and it is killing the church while claiming it is "saving Christianity." A few years ago, the cover of *Newsweek*'s Easter issue blared in red letters, "The Decline and Fall of Christian America." In 2015, the Daily Beast website asked, "Does Christianity Have a Future?" As our culture wobbles wildly on its spiritual axis, many are asking whether Christianity can survive in the twenty-first century.

Some are asking whether we need to reinvent Christianity in order to save it.

My friend, I have written this book to declare to you that people need saving, our society needs saving, our nation needs saving, and our world needs saving—*but Christianity does not need to be saved.*

In the pages that follow, I will show you, candidly and clearly, with abundant evidence, that the only harm that can ever come to the gospel or to the church of Jesus Christ comes from those who are trying to "save" Christianity by reinventing it and distorting it beyond recognition.

From the first century to the twenty-first century, the greatest threat to Christianity has never come from the outside—from persecution, atheism, the godless culture, or opposing religions. In fact, *external* attacks have historically strengthened and purified the church.

The greatest threats to the church have always been *internal.* The greatest threats have come from those who claim to be Christians, who are leaders in the church, but whose teachings and doctrines are at odds with God's Word. Satan is working overtime to destroy the church from within. It's always an inside job. Many once-evangelical churches are now filled with the unsaved, the uncommitted, and the unconverted. As the church goes, so goes society.

Some false teachers started in the evangelical Christian community but left to form "progressive Christian" communities or "emerging" churches. But many others are still inside the evangelical church, or teaching at evangelical colleges, universities, and seminaries. They are poisoning the

Bible-believing church from within. I want to alert you and arm you with vital information so that you can discern the essentials of the Christian faith as set forth in the Bible. I want you to recognize false teachers and false doctrines when you see them. I don't want you to be fooled.

In the great commission, Jesus commanded the church to evangelize and convert the world for him. Today, the world is converting the church on behalf of Satan, the god of this world. When churches and church leaders corrupt "the faith that was once for all entrusted to God's holy people,"[1] they are cooperating in the destruction of the church, sowing seeds of spiritual death. God's Word is the true light for all of humanity, especially for us as twenty-first-century Christians, living in these chaotic times.

These leaders who think they are saving Christianity by deconstructing God's truth are in fact the greatest danger the church faces today. Though I don't doubt their good intentions, I believe that Satan is using them as willing marks to destroy the church from within. And that's why, when speaking of those who identify themselves as "progressive" or "emerging," I deliberately place the word *Christians* in quotation marks. Please understand, I am not judging these people as unsaved. God alone knows the status of their souls. But to me, the word *Christian* has a specific definition that these progressive "Christians" don't meet—by their own declaration. And I simply cannot in good conscience refer to people as Christians who treat God's Word as an untrustworthy and unreliable narrative, and who deny the truth of John 3:16 and John 14:6.

Accordingly, I have five goals in writing this book:

1. To expose the false teaching that is destroying the church from within.
2. To renew your confidence in the God of the Bible and in Jesus Christ, his only Son.
3. To renew your confidence in the future of the church and the central role it plays in human history.
4. To promote peace, unity, and understanding in the body of Christ by appealing to these false teachers to repent of their error.
5. To present the essential, biblical, nonnegotiable tenets of authentic Christianity, the doctrines I call "mere faith." This is the original faith God entrusted to us in his Word—a faith that must never be exchanged for the lies of this fallen world.

The good news is that the historic gospel of Jesus Christ is still the Good News. The good news is that there are sound, biblical answers to the questions and doubts raised by postmodern, post-evangelical, progressive "Christians." The good news is that we do not have to wander in a fog of uncertainty about God's Word and God's Son. The good news is that God is still in control of history, and Jesus is still the way, the truth, and the life.

✝

PART ONE

THE SLIDE
TOWARD
COMPROMISE

A Short History of Spiritual Defection

Charles Templeton was a twenty-year-old sports cartoonist for the Toronto *Globe and Mail* when he decided to follow Jesus Christ. In 1941, when he was twenty-five, Templeton founded Toronto's Avenue Road Church of the Nazarene and served as the church's pastor—despite never having attended seminary. The church grew and thrived under his leadership.

Four years later, he met Chicago pastor Torrey Johnson at a gathering of Christian youth leaders in Winona Lake, Indiana, and the two formed an organization they called Youth for Christ International (YFC). The new evangelistic organization hired a fiery young preacher named Billy Graham as its first full-time evangelist.

Templeton conducted many evangelistic meetings for YFC, and thousands of young people came to Christ through his preaching. But he began experiencing doubts about the Bible and doubts about his calling as an evangelist. After all, he had no formal training. Templeton decided to enroll at Princeton to study the Bible and theology in a more structured way.

At Princeton, Templeton encountered liberal theology for the first time. His instructors challenged his thinking and his faith. He came away believing that the Bible is a flawed document, written by fallible people. He no longer considered it the living Word of God. He concluded that science, not the Bible, held the answers to humanity's questions and problems.

Through correspondence and personal conversations, Charles Templeton began to challenge his friend Billy Graham. Templeton asked Graham tough theological questions. He tried to convince him that the Bible was untrustworthy. As a result, Graham's own doubts began to grow.

In 1949, Billy Graham received an invitation from Henrietta Mears to speak at the Forest Home conference center in Southern California. Mears was an influential Bible teacher who mentored Bill and Vonette Bright (founders of Campus Crusade), Jim Rayburn (founder of Young Life), and Louis Evans Jr. (pastor of Bel Air Church). But Graham was reluctant to accept the invitation. Fresh from an evangelism effort in Pennsylvania that he felt had gone poorly, and with his faith under assault from his friend Charles Templeton, Graham's confidence was at a low ebb. How could he preach the gospel from a Bible he no longer trusted with full certainty?

Despite his doubts, Billy Graham accepted the invitation to Forest Home, and while he was there he immersed himself in the Scriptures. As he read and meditated on the Bible, he encountered one phrase again and again: "Thus saith the Lord." He realized that this one phrase, reverberating throughout Scripture, was working on his heart, calling him to a conviction that the Bible truly is God's divinely inspired, eternal, powerful Word.

One night during his stay at Forest Home, while on a solitary stroll in the woods, Graham set his Bible on a stump and knelt before it as a makeshift prayer altar. "O God!" he called out. "There are many things in this book I do not understand." He confessed in prayer that he had no answer for many of the questions his friend Charles Templeton had raised. But the Holy Spirit moved him to say, "Father, I am going to accept this as Thy Word—by *faith!* I'm going to allow faith to go beyond my intellectual questions and doubts, and I will believe this to be Your inspired Word."[1]

The next day, Billy Graham spoke at a conference meeting, and four hundred people responded by committing their lives to Christ. Henrietta Mears said that Graham "preached with authority" in a way she hadn't seen in him before that night.[2]

Beginning in late September 1949, Billy Graham led the historic Los Angeles Crusade under a circus tent dubbed the Canvas Cathedral. The crusade, originally planned to last three weeks, was held over for an additional five weeks as the nightly crowds began to swell. Graham believed that everything God accomplished through his ministry could be traced to the night he set his Bible on a tree stump at Forest Home and accepted it as God's inspired Word.[3]

Years later, Charles Templeton said this of his lost friendship with Billy Graham: "I disagree with him at almost every point in his views on God and Christianity and think that much of what he says in the pulpit is puerile, archaic nonsense. But there is no feigning in Billy Graham: he believes what he believes with an invincible innocence. He is the only mass-evangelist I would trust. And I miss him."[4]

Though Templeton and Graham no longer had a shared faith in common, they remained on friendly terms. In 1996, five years before his death, Charles Templeton wrote his autobiography—which bore the tragic title of *Farewell to God: My Reasons for Rejecting the Christian Faith*—in which he recalled a conversation he had with Billy Graham after the two had parted ways theologically:

> In the course of our conversation, I said, "But, Billy, it's simply not possible any longer to believe, for instance, the biblical account of creation. . . ."
>
> "I don't accept that," Billy said. "And there are reputable scholars who don't."
>
> "Who are these scholars?' I said. "Men in conservative Christian colleges?"
>
> "Most of them, yes," he said. "But that's not the point. I believe the Genesis account of creation because it's in the Bible. I've discovered something

in my ministry: when I take the Bible literally, when I proclaim it as the Word of God, my preaching has power. When I stand on the platform and say, 'God says,' or 'The Bible says,' the Holy Spirit uses me. There are results. Wiser men than you or I have been arguing questions like this for centuries. . . . I've decided, once for all, to stop questioning and accept the Bible as God's Word."

"But, Billy," I protested, "you can't do that. You don't dare stop thinking about the most important question in life. Do it and you begin to die. It's intellectual suicide."

"I don't know about anybody else," he said, "but I've decided that that's the path for me."[5]

Shortly before Templeton's death, he sat for an interview with Christian journalist Lee Strobel. Templeton was in his eighties and in the early stages of Alzheimer's disease, though he was still able to communicate "with eloquence and enthusiasm."[6] Strobel asked him for his assessment of Jesus of Nazareth. Templeton seemed melancholy and almost nostalgic as he said that Jesus was "the greatest human being who has ever lived. He was a moral genius. His ethical sense was unique. . . . What could one say about him except that this was a form of greatness? . . . Everything good I know, everything decent I know, everything pure I know, I learned from Jesus. Yes . . . yes. And tough! Just look at Jesus. He castigated people. He was angry. People don't think of him that way, but they don't read the Bible. He had a righteous anger. He cared for the oppressed and exploited. There's no question that he had the highest moral standard, the least duplicity, the greatest compassion, of any human being in history."[7]

Then, his eyes flooding with tears, Templeton concluded, "And if I may put it this way, *I . . . miss . . . him.*" Then Charles Templeton wept.

After a few moments, he composed himself, dismissively waved his hand, and said with embarrassment, "Enough of that."[8]

Here was a man who had once been an evangelist, passionately devoted to sharing the Good News of Jesus Christ. But he had defected from the faith and become a propagandist for atheism. Yet, near the end of his life, he wept over his lost friendship with Jesus.

I wish I could say that this is the most tragic story I've ever heard. Unfortunately, it's an all-too-common story. The pattern of Charles Templeton's life has played out countless times, in millions of lost souls, ever since the human race began.

Spiritual Defection in the Old Testament

The first spiritual defection in history began the moment that Eve listened to the words of the serpent: "Did God really say . . . ?"[9] Since then, the story of humanity has been one of apostasy, of abandoning or falling away from God and his truth.

Both the Old Testament nation of Israel and the New Testament church were constantly menaced by false teachings that sprang up and infected the congregation like a plague. Throughout the Scriptures, God warns his people against the danger of spiritual defection. For example, in Deuteronomy 6, God urges his people to love him and to have nothing to do with other gods. The Israelites were to meditate on God's Word, and to teach God's commands to their children when they lay down at night and when they arose in the morning. They were never to forget that God had liberated them from slavery and had blessed them in the land. But time after time, Israel ignored God's warnings and fell into apostasy and idolatry.

After Israel's exodus out of Egypt, Moses led the people to the foot of Mount Sinai. He climbed the mountain, and there he received the stone tablets on which God had written the Ten Commandments. But while Moses was on the mountain, some of the people made an idol of a golden calf. When Moses returned to the camp, he found the people worshiping the idol they had made. He angrily broke the tablets and punished the idolaters.

Many years later, after Israel conquered the Promised Land under Joshua's leadership, the people of Israel became spiritually complacent. Once again, they drifted into idol worship and rebellion against God. This was the time of the judges, when the twelve tribes of Israel had no central government and no moral leadership. Judges 17:6 tells us, "In those days Israel had no king; all the people did whatever seemed right in their own eyes."[10]

Throughout the book of Judges, the twelve tribes of Israel follow a cyclical pattern of spiritual renewal followed by spiritual defection and idolatry. Whenever the Israelites began following the depraved practices of their ungodly neighbors, such as the Canaanites, Philistines, and Assyrians, God would send an enemy nation to terrorize and oppress them. In their panic and suffering, the Israelites would suddenly take God's commandments seriously. They would cry out to God for deliverance from their enemies, and God would hear their prayers and send them a deliverer. These deliverers—people such as Deborah, Gideon, and Samson—were known as judges, who would deliver the Israelites in their hour of need. But as soon as the enemy nation was driven off, the people would again become spiritually complacent and disobedient—and the cycle of spiritual defection and idolatry would begin once more.

The book of 1 Samuel introduces us to Samuel, the last of the judges and the first of the biblical prophets. He would later anoint both Saul and David, the first two kings of Israel. The book of 1 Samuel contains these sobering words: "In those days the word of the LORD was rare; there were not many visions."[11] Because the people had defected from God, he was silent and he sent them no visions, no word to guide them.

Under the leadership of King David and his son and successor King Solomon, the city of Jerusalem and its great Temple became the headquarters for worship of the one true God. The kingdom of Israel experienced a golden age under Solomon's godly leadership—at least, for most of his life. Solomon started out well, building and dedicating the great Temple to the worship of the Lord. But his story eventually became a case study in the tragic consequences of spiritual defection, and the latter years of his reign were overshadowed by apostasy. Scripture records how Solomon's heart was led astray:

> King Solomon, however, loved many foreign women besides Pharaoh's daughter—Moabites, Ammonites, Edomites, Sidonians and Hittites. They were from nations about which the LORD had told the Israelites, "You must not intermarry with them, because they will surely turn your hearts after their gods." Nevertheless, Solomon held fast to them in love. He had seven hundred wives of royal birth and three hundred concubines, and his wives led him astray.[12]

Many Bible scholars believe that Solomon wrote the book of Ecclesiastes later in life, perhaps after recognizing his spiritual error and repenting of it. That might explain these words:

> I find more bitter than death
> the woman who is a snare,
> whose heart is a trap
> and whose hands are chains.
> The man who pleases God will escape her,
> but the sinner she will ensnare.[13]

God's warning against being led into apostasy by our lusts or our false friends is reinforced by the apostle Paul in the New Testament: "Do not be yoked together with unbelievers.

For what do righteousness and wickedness have in common? Or what fellowship can light have with darkness?"[14]

Solomon's spiritual defection undoubtedly affected his moral, spiritual, and political leadership of the nation of Israel. As Solomon's heart was turned away from God, so were the hearts of the people. Solomon allowed pagan idols and temples to be built in honor of demonic gods and goddesses like Ashtoreth, Chemosh, and Molek.[15] The worship of these false gods was associated with gruesome child sacrifices and obscene sexual acts. As Solomon went, so went the nation of Israel.

After Solomon died and Rehoboam became king, the kingdom of Israel was divided by tribal conflict. Ten tribes broke away and formed the northern kingdom of Israel, with its capital at Shechem (and later at Samaria). The other two tribes, Judah and Benjamin, formed the southern kingdom of Judah, with its capital at Jerusalem. After the split, both kingdoms eventually defected from God and turned to idol worship.

The most important prophet in the northern kingdom was Elijah, who lived in the ninth century BC during the reign of wicked King Ahab and Queen Jezebel, the daughter of the king of Sidon. It was a time of heartbreaking apostasy as the people were led into the worship of Baal by their corrupted king and pagan queen. At Mount Carmel, Elijah set up a contest between himself (as a prophet of God) and the priests of Baal, in which both sides prepared a sacrifice and called upon their respective deities to send fire to consume their sacrifice.

From morning until evening, the pagan priests prayed and

wailed and cut themselves with knives, but Baal remained silent. When at last Elijah called upon the Lord, fire immediately rained down from heaven and consumed the sacrifice. Having defeated the false priests, Elijah ordered their execution.

When Queen Jezebel heard what had happened, she placed a bounty on Elijah's head, sending him fleeing for his life into the wilderness. There he took refuge in a cave.

In 1 Kings 19:9, the Lord appears to Elijah in the cave and asks, "What are you doing here, Elijah?"

Discouraged and lonely, Elijah replies, "I have been very zealous for the LORD God Almighty. The Israelites have rejected your covenant, torn down your altars, and put your prophets to death with the sword. I am the only one left, and now they are trying to kill me too."[16] Elijah honestly believed that he was the only believer left in all of Israel.

The Lord sent Elijah out on a mountain and showed him a series of powerful events. A mighty wind shattered mountains and rocks—but the Lord was not in the wind. Then came fire and an earthquake, but the Lord was not in the fire nor was he in the earthquake. Then Elijah heard a gentle whisper—and he knew that the Lord was in that soft whisper.[17]

Sometimes God acts dramatically, as when he sent fire from heaven in response to Elijah's prayer. But God's greatest power most often is demonstrated in a gentle whisper, the still, small voice of his Word. Through the Word of God, the Spirit of God speaks to the human heart, bringing a change to the heart's attitude while redirecting the human will.

Even though it seemed as if all of Israel had fallen into apostasy and idolatry, God wanted Elijah to know that there was still a faithful remnant in Israel who had heard the gentle whisper of God's Word. God told Elijah, "I reserve seven thousand in Israel—all whose knees have not bowed down to Baal and whose mouths have not kissed him."[18]

Despite Elijah's victory on Mount Carmel and his warning to the people, the northern kingdom continued to drift away from God. Finally, in 722 BC, after a three-year siege, the Assyrians conquered Samaria and took the ten tribes of the northern kingdom into captivity in Assyria. There, the tribes were absorbed into the surrounding pagan culture and never returned to the Promised Land. They are known to history as the ten lost tribes of Israel.

Even when it seems that we're surrounded by apostates and enemies, even when it seems we're alone and that everyone around us has defected, we must remember God's message to Elijah. Listen for the gentle whisper of the Spirit. Remember that God always reserves a remnant of faithful followers for himself. Therefore, stand strong in your faithfulness to the Lord, so that you will always be counted among God's faithful remnant.

Spiritual Defection Leads to Enslavement

Apostasy was also rampant in the southern kingdom of Judah. The spiritual life of the nation hit bottom during the era of the prophet Jeremiah. He warned the leaders and the people of Judah that destruction and enslavement awaited them if they did not repent of their idolatry.

God was amazingly patient with Judah. Jeremiah preached

and warned the nation for about forty years—a period that spanned the reign of five kings: Josiah, Jehoahaz, Jehoiakim, Jehoiachin, and Zedekiah. Yet the people not only worshiped the Phoenician god Baal and the Hittite goddess Asherah, they even sacrificed their own innocent children to the Canaanite demon-god Molek.

God spoke to Jeremiah and gave him a message for the nation. The essence of God's warning to Judah is summed up in these words:

"Your wickedness will punish you;
   your backsliding will rebuke you.
Consider then and realize
   how evil and bitter it is for you
when you forsake the LORD your God
   and have no awe of me,"
declares the Lord, the LORD Almighty.[19]

In the Septuagint—the ancient Greek translation of the Old Testament, written about two hundred years before Christ—the word translated "backsliding" in English is *apostasia* in Greek, from which we get the word *apostasy*. In his message through Jeremiah, God identifies the cause of the backsliding and spiritual defection that plagued the nation: The people had no awe (or fear) of God.

During the time of Elijah, God had reserved to himself a remnant of seven thousand followers. But during the time of Jeremiah, the faithful prophet stood almost entirely alone in his effort to awaken the people to their impending doom.

Jeremiah had only two allies who served God as faithfully as he did—Baruch the scribe and an Ethiopian eunuch named Ebed-Melek.[20]

From a human perspective, Jeremiah spent forty years wasting his breath. Not a single person turned to God in repentance. Finally, the officials of King Zedekiah seized him, threw him in a cistern filled with mud, and left him to die. Jeremiah was rescued from the cistern by Ebed-Melek, though he remained in captivity until the Babylonian army captured Jerusalem in 587 BC. The Babylonians destroyed the city and slaughtered or enslaved most of the people (just as God had warned), but they set Jeremiah free.

After seventy years in captivity under the Babylonians and the Persians (who conquered the Babylonians), the Israelites were set free by a decree of the Persian king Cyrus the Great. The book of Nehemiah describes how, under Nehemiah's leadership, the Jews returned to Jerusalem and rebuilt the city walls that had been destroyed by the Babylonians. Nehemiah 8 tells the story of a revival that swept the nation, but by chapter 13, the people of Jerusalem have already become spiritually lukewarm and are drifting toward apostasy again.

Between the end of the Old Testament and the beginning of the New, the nation of Israel had fallen into such a wretched spiritual state that when the long-awaited Messiah finally appeared, the leaders and the people didn't accept him. From the beginning to the end of his public ministry, Jesus faced constant opposition and threats from the very religious leaders who should have recognized him from the messianic prophecies of the Old Testament and welcomed him.

Spiritual Defection in the New Testament

In the New Testament, we see apostasy in the lives of the people who crowded around Jesus as he walked and taught and preached the gospel of the Kingdom. John 6 vividly illustrates how spiritual defection works. First, the apostle John tells us that "a great crowd of people followed [Jesus] because they saw the signs he had performed by healing the sick."[21] People were attracted by the miracles of Jesus, including the feeding of the five thousand.[22]

Later, when Jesus crossed the Sea of Galilee to Capernaum on the opposite shore, the crowds tracked him down. There, Jesus told them:

> Very truly I tell you, you are looking for me, not because you saw the signs I performed but because you ate the loaves and had your fill. Do not work for food that spoils, but for food that endures to eternal life, which the Son of Man will give you. For on him God the Father has placed his seal of approval. . . . I am the bread of life. Whoever comes to me will never go hungry, and whoever believes in me will never be thirsty. But as I told you, you have seen me and still you do not believe.[23]

Jesus was talking to people who followed him, who were excited about him, who were eager to receive things from him, but who did not believe in him. They wanted the bread he provided at the feeding of the five thousand, but they would not receive *him* as the everlasting Bread of Life. They showed up, hoping he would work miracles, but they didn't want to hear the truth he proclaimed. They wanted his social gospel—the free food distribution—but they didn't want his spiritual gospel, the food that would endure to eternal life.

After these followers listened to Jesus preach about himself—for example, "Whoever eats my flesh and drinks my blood has eternal life, and I will raise them up at the last day. For my flesh is real food and my blood is real drink. Whoever eats my flesh and drinks my blood remains in me, and I in them"[24]—many of them said, "This is a hard teaching. Who can accept it?"[25]

Then John records a sad commentary on these disappointed followers: "From this time many of his disciples turned back and no longer followed him."[26] In other words, they defected. They fell into apostasy.

Only a small, faithful band of followers remained after the rest turned away. They stayed not because Jesus performed miracles and fed the masses, but because they believed in the Good News of eternal life through faith in him. When Jesus asked the twelve disciples if they too wanted to leave him, Simon Peter summed up their faith in these words: "Lord, to whom shall we go? You have the words of eternal life. We have come to believe and to know that you are the Holy One of God."[27]

When we speak of apostasy or defection from the Christian faith, we are referring to those who reject the claims of Jesus Christ. Many people approve of Jesus, say nice things about

Jesus, and perhaps even try to follow his moral teachings, yet they reject what he taught about himself and who he is. Even some atheists claim to admire the moral teachings of Jesus while rejecting his claims. For example, biologist and well-known spokesman for atheism Richard Dawkins writes, "Jesus, if he existed . . . was surely one of the great ethical innovators of history. The Sermon on the Mount is way ahead of its time. His 'turn the other cheek' anticipated Gandhi and Martin Luther King by two thousand years."[28] But Jesus didn't come to earth to be a "great ethical innovator," and to be an admirer of his is not the same as being a believer and a follower.

Sadly, there are even many pastors, theologians, and writers who call themselves Christians yet reject the claims of Christ. But anyone who purports to follow Jesus while rejecting his claims is a defector and an apostate. The people who followed Jesus around first-century Judea and Galilee, marveled at his miracles, and ate the bread he broke, but walked away from his teachings about himself, were apostate. And the people today who want us to follow Jesus' moral and social teachings while denying his claims about himself are equally apostate.

What Did Jesus Claim about Himself?

When Jesus told the crowds that had gathered who he was, they were shocked—and many were offended. Here was this nobody from nowhere, this carpenter's son from Nazareth, proclaiming in his backwoods Galilean accent that he was the long-awaited Messiah and equal to God himself! The claims Jesus made were so specific and so shocking that many people today—including many who say they are Christians—still find them offensive and try to downplay them or ignore them.

What are these claims that are so provocative?

Jesus said he came from heaven and that he existed eternally.[29] He said he was sent into the world by God the Father.[30] He claimed to be eternally coexistent with God the Father, even before the creation of the world.[31] He claimed to be the Savior of the world; the way, the truth, and the life; and the only way to God the Father.[32]

Further, he claimed to be the Messiah long promised in the Old Testament Scriptures.[33] He claimed to be the resurrection and the life.[34] According to Scripture, it was the Spirit of God who caused Mary, the mother of Jesus, to become pregnant while a virgin.[35] At Jesus' baptism, both God the Father and the Holy Spirit affirmed him to be the Son of God.[36] His claim to deity was confirmed by both Old Testament prophecy and the New Testament fulfillment of that prophecy—a prophecy that Jesus would be called *Immanuel*, meaning, "God with us."[37]

Jesus claimed the right *as God* to be worshiped by humanity, and the right to judge the human race.[38] Jesus claimed to be without sin.[39] Jesus claimed—and demonstrated—divine authority over disease, death, the wind and waves, and demonic spirits.[40] Jesus claimed to have the power and authority to rise from the dead.[41] He claimed the authority to forgive sins, an authority that belongs to God alone.[42]

When Peter told Jesus, "You are the Messiah, the Son of

the living God," Jesus blessed him and told him, "This was not revealed to you by flesh and blood, but by my Father in heaven."[43] Yet the religious leaders, hearing these same claims, plotted to kill Jesus because "he was even calling God his own Father, making himself equal with God."[44] He claimed to be equal *with* God and eternal *as* God. In short, he claimed to *be* God.[45] The religious leaders understood that if the claims of Jesus were untrue, they were blasphemous.

This is the same reasoning C. S. Lewis followed when he formulated his so-called trilemma (or three-sided problem) in *Mere Christianity*:

> I am trying here to prevent anyone saying the really foolish thing that people often say about Him: "I'm ready to accept Jesus as a great moral teacher, but I don't accept His claim to be God." That is the one thing we must not say. A man who was merely a man and said the sort of things Jesus said would not be a great moral teacher. He would either be a lunatic— on a level with the man who says he is a poached egg—or else he would be the Devil of Hell. You must make your choice. Either this man was, and is, the Son of God; or else a madman or something worse. You can shut Him up for a fool, you can spit at Him and kill Him as a demon; or you can fall at His feet and call Him Lord and God. But let us not come with any patronizing nonsense about His being a great human teacher. He has not left that open to us. He did not intend to.[46]

Some have misunderstood the point of Lewis's trilemma, saying it doesn't prove that Jesus was who he claimed to be. Of course it doesn't. Lewis wasn't trying to *prove* anything by his statement. He simply wanted us to understand that we can't have it both ways. We can't say, "Jesus was a great moral teacher, but he was not the Son of God." We can't say, "Jesus was a great social reformer, but he is not the only way to God the Father." We can't say, "I'm a Christian, but I don't believe in Jesus as my Lord and Savior." We cannot cherry-pick the teachings of Jesus, selecting the ones that fit our political and social biases while ignoring his claim to be the Savior and the only way to God the Father.

If Jesus was a deliberate liar, he could not be a great moral teacher. If he was merely a human being who *thought* he was God, he would not be a great moral teacher; he would be delusional, and all his teachings would be unreliable and tainted by madness and megalomania. If you reject Jesus' claims to be sinless, to be eternally existent, to be God in human flesh, to have authority to both forgive and judge human beings—if you reject all that, you have no basis for accepting *anything else* that Jesus said. And you have no basis for calling yourself a Christian.

You might ask, "How do we know that Jesus really said everything attributed to him in the Bible? Maybe the Sermon on the Mount is accurate but John 3:16 is not. Why can't we just follow our favorite sayings of Jesus and ignore the ones we don't like?" The answer is obvious. By doing so, we are not following Jesus. We are merely using Jesus to rubber-stamp our own biases, preferences, and moral weaknesses. We are trying to conform Jesus to our own image instead of conforming ourselves to his. The Gospels are the only objective basis we have for verifying the words of Jesus, and the Gospel accounts are harmonious and reliable. Reject *anything* that Jesus said about himself and we forfeit any claim to be his followers.

It's the entire gospel or none at all—that's the choice Jesus set before us. All or nothing, take it or leave it. Believe everything he said and organize your life around it, or go your own way. Either Jesus is God, as he says he is, or he's a liar or a lunatic. Those are your only three options. Choose carefully. But don't try to remake Jesus into something more comfortable. As Lewis said, Jesus has not left that option open to us. He didn't intend to.

Remember these defining words of Jesus: "If you hold to my teaching, you are really my disciples. Then you will know the truth, and the truth will set you free."[47] But if you choose *not* to hold to his teachings—*all* of them—where does that leave you? If you reject *any* of his teachings, how can you call yourself a Christian?

Insulate Yourself against Apostasy

When someone comes to faith in Jesus Christ and makes a commitment to him as Lord and Savior, that change of heart is called *conversion*. Authentic conversion means more than merely agreeing with a set of creeds or doctrines *about* Jesus. It means accepting his lordship. It means a humble and absolute surrender of the will to Jesus.

Once a person has experienced that change of heart

and has accepted the lordship and authority of Jesus Christ over his or her life, any later rejection of Jesus' lordship and authority becomes an act of defection, rebellion, or falling away. Apostasy is a willful departure from biblical Christian faith. It is the opposite of conversion.

Now, does this mean that we, as Christians, can lose our salvation? No! God's grace to us is an unearned, unmerited gift. Thanks be to God, he never reneges on his gift to those who truly believe.

"But," you may ask, "what about Charles Templeton? After coming to Christ, after founding and pastoring a church, after cofounding Youth for Christ and preaching on the same platform with Billy Graham, after leading many people to the Lord, didn't he defect from the faith? Didn't he die in unbelief? Didn't he lose his salvation?" These are good questions, and there are no simple answers. But there *are* sound, biblical answers.

First, we don't know the state of Charles Templeton's heart when he died. We know that, not long before his death, he told Lee Strobel that he still admired Jesus—and he missed Jesus. God alone knows whether Templeton died in a state of belief or a state of unbelief and condemnation. God knows, and he rightly judges the heart.

Second, we don't know the state of Charles Templeton's heart when he made his original profession of faith. Was his faith genuine? Again, only God knows. We cannot claim to know.

But one thing we *do* know is what Jesus taught us: "I have come down from heaven not to do my will but to do the will of him who sent me. And this is the will of him who sent me, *that I shall lose none of all those he has given me*, but raise them up at the last day."[48]

The Scriptures tell us that God "predestined us for adoption to sonship through Jesus Christ, in accordance with his pleasure and will."[49] The Scriptures also say that "those he predestined, he also called; those he called, he also justified; those he justified, he also glorified."[50] From a human perspective, we make the decision to receive Jesus as Lord and Savior of our own free will. But from a heavenly perspective, the reason we make that choice is because *God first chose us.*

If God the Father called and chose Charles Templeton and gave him to Jesus the Son, then Charles Templeton is saved, justified, and glorified with Christ. But if Charles Templeton died unsaved and in a state of unbelief, then God the Father never called, chose, or gave Charles Templeton to Jesus the Son in the first place.

That is why the apostle Peter urges us, "Therefore, my brothers and sisters, make every effort to confirm your calling and election. For if you do these things, you will never stumble."[51] Don't take your salvation for granted. Don't assume that because you "made a decision" for Christ way back when that you are truly saved. Heed the example of Charles Templeton and take it as a warning. I would hate for you to come to the end of your life and confess through tears, as he did, "I miss Jesus!" Make sure that God has truly called you and chosen you by remaining faithful to the end. If you do that, the Bible promises, you will never fall away from the faith.

How can we remain faithful to God, who loves us so generously and freely? The book of Jude tells us how to walk faithfully with God throughout our days.

First, *remain faithful by knowing God's truth and by being skeptical of false doctrines.* Jude writes, "Dear friends, remember what the apostles of our Lord Jesus Christ foretold. They said to you, 'In the last times there will be scoffers who will follow their own ungodly desires.' These are the people who divide you, who follow mere natural instincts and do not have the Spirit."[52] Steep yourself in the Word of God and test every teaching against Scripture. Be on guard against falsehood and smooth talk and those who offer some new twist on Christianity. Don't accept any "new" gospel—the emerging gospel, the social gospel, the prosperity gospel, or any other gospel—as a substitute for the *true* gospel of salvation by grace through faith.

Second, *insulate yourself against unbelief* "by building yourselves up in your most holy faith and praying in the Holy Spirit."[53] Set aside time to develop a deep intimacy with God and his Word. Spend time alone with the Bible. Books and sermons cannot take the place of feeding directly on the Word of God. Also, linger with God in prayer. Never let anything—not even your family or ministry—take the place of time alone with God. If you neglect your time with God, your spiritual life will wither and dry up. You won't lose your salvation, but you will almost certainly miss out on the blessings God wants to pour into your life.

When the prodigal son wandered away from his father, he did not lose his father's love, but he suffered terribly. He missed out on the blessings of living closely and intimately with his father. The prodigal son forfeited the joy of daily experiencing the warmth of his father's love. When you spend time away from your heavenly Father, you will inevitably suffer. You'll suffer mental anguish and emotional despondency. You'll suffer the painful consequences of the bad choices you make when you cut yourself off from God's wisdom and guidance. So insulate yourself against unbelief by spending time in prayer and in God's Word.

Third, *insulate yourself against bad influences*. Especially beware of those who know the truth but have turned their backs on it. After Charles Templeton turned his back on Christianity, he argued with Billy Graham and tried to convince Billy to turn away from Jesus as well. In fact, Templeton's persistent attacks on the Bible triggered a crisis of doubt that Billy Graham could resolve only by praying a prayer of committed faith.

The Scriptures warn, "It is impossible for those who have once been enlightened, who have tasted the heavenly gift, who have shared in the Holy Spirit, who have tasted the goodness of the word of God and the powers of the coming age and who have fallen away, to be brought back to repentance. To their loss they are crucifying the Son of God all over again and subjecting him to public disgrace."[54] Beware those who have fallen away and want to drag you down with them.

Fourth, *insulate yourself from falsehood by boldly sharing the truth with others*. Be a witness to those who are outside the church. Be a teacher and an encourager to those who are inside the church. Jude tells us, "Be merciful to those who doubt; save others by snatching them from the fire; to others show mercy, mixed with fear—hating even the clothing stained by corrupted flesh."[55]

When struggling believers share their doubts with you, don't shame them or make them feel guilty for doubting. Be merciful and kind, but teach them the truth about God's Word and God's Son. Pray for wisdom and God's love, and then speak the truth to them in love. When you encounter people who are outside the faith, don't be embarrassed, shy, or afraid to tell them, "God loves you and sent his Son, Jesus, to die for you. He wants to take away your guilt and sin, and he wants to be your Father and your friend forever."

When was the last time you shared Christ with someone? Are you involved in the lives of lost and hurting people? Is your heart moved by the many unsaved people in the world around you? The more often you share God's love with others, the less likely you will be to lapse into error and fall away from the truth.

Jude closes his letter with a beautiful and reassuring hymn of praise to God, the one who will never let us fall out of his grace: "To him who is able to keep you from stumbling and to present you before his glorious presence without fault and with great joy—to the only God our Savior be glory, majesty, power and authority, through Jesus Christ our Lord, before all ages, now and forevermore! Amen."[56]

The Lord is able to keep you from falling. He has called you and chosen you, and he will not let you go. Make sure you don't let go of him.

Destroying Christianity by "Saving" It

On May 4, 2019, popular author, speaker, and blogger Rachel Held Evans died at the age of thirty-seven. She left behind a husband and two children, ages three and almost one. *Washington Post* religion reporter Sarah Pulliam Bailey eulogized Evans as "a best-selling Christian author who was unafraid to wade into fierce theological battles over issues such as the role of women, science, LGBT issues and politics on her blog and social media."[1]

Evans had gone into the hospital in mid-April for treatment of an infection and the flu. Her condition worsened when an allergic reaction to antibiotics sent her into seizures. The doctors placed her in a medically induced coma, but when they tried to wean her off the drugs, she suffered a fatal swelling of the brain. It was a terrible tragedy, and my heart aches for her family.

Evans had gained a following as a blogger in the early 2000s. When her evangelical home church in Dayton, Tennessee, became active in the battle against same-sex marriage, she left and joined an Episcopal church. In her writings, she questioned a literal reading of God's Word and encouraged women to take more prominent leadership roles in the church. Witty and charming, she became a sought-after speaker at conferences.

In *A Year of Biblical Womanhood: How a Liberated Woman Found Herself Sitting on Her Roof, Covering Her Head, and Calling Her Husband "Master,"* Evans records how she spent a year practicing the teachings of the Bible as literally as possible. Her book is funny and provocative, and features interviews with people from several faith traditions. However, it soon becomes clear that, although she genuinely loves the Bible as a historical and cultural document—as a collection of powerful stories—she does not believe the Bible should be trusted as a guide for Christian faith and Christian living. For example, she writes,

> So far, the first two months of my "radical experiment" had been far from radical. . . . Up until this point, I'd managed to avoid the fact that I'd planned a year of my life around a collection of ancient texts that routinely describe women as property.
>
> It was time for a reality check.

Despite what some may claim, the Bible's not the best place to look for traditional family values as we understand them today. The text predates our Western construct of the nuclear family and presents us with a familial culture closer to that of a third-world country (or a TLC reality show) than that of Ward and June Cleaver.[2]

If indeed it is time for a reality check, it should be noted that Evans's conclusions are simply not true. God is the one who designed the nuclear family (see Genesis 2–4), and Eve was not Adam's "property." In fact, in Adam's own words, she was "bone of my bones and flesh of my flesh."[3] The fact that later generations in the Bible practiced polygamy, had concubines, and distorted the family pattern that God originally devised does not mean that the nuclear family—one dad, one mom, and some number of children—is a "Western construct."

Later in the book, she calls the Bible "a sacred collection of letters and laws, poetry and proverbs, philosophy and prophecies, written and assembled over thousands of years in cultures and contexts very different from our own, that tells the complex, ever-unfolding story of God's interaction with humanity."[4] This definition of the Bible is accurate but incomplete. Evans avoids stating that the Bible is the Word of God, written by human beings under the direct inspiration of the Holy Spirit.[5] By calling the Bible "sacred" while denying that it is God's inspired Word, she can claim to respect and venerate the Bible while rejecting any biblical teachings she disagrees with. She goes on to write:

For those who count the Bible as sacred, interpretation is not a matter of *whether* to pick and choose, but *how* to pick and choose. We are all selective. We all wrestle with how to interpret and apply the Bible to our lives. We all go to the text looking for something, and we all have a tendency to find it. So the question we have to ask ourselves is this: Are we reading with the prejudice of love or are we reading with the prejudices of judgment and power, self-interest and greed?[6]

This excerpt highlights a common form of argument among progressive, postmodern "Christians." They offer a false choice between two options: Do you want to interpret the Bible in a loving way, or do you want to interpret the Bible in a selfish and judgmental way? In other words, if you don't interpret the Bible as Evans does, you must be motivated by greedy self-interest. As if those are the only two options.

There seem to be many today who are swayed by this unfair form of argument. After all, who wouldn't prefer "the prejudice of love" over evil intentions? But let me offer a third option: As sincere, loving, Bible-believing Christians, can we not choose to read the Bible with an attitude of obedience to the authority of God's Word? Can we not read simply because we want to know what God's Word says so we can obey God—nothing more, nothing less?

The tendency of many progressives to undermine the veracity of God's Word seems to be an attempt to rationalize the practice of cherry-picking the Scriptures according to their personal biases and ideologies. "The prejudice of love" is a clever turn of phrase, but it's not a sound argument for rejecting the authority and integrity of Scripture. Evans refers to the Bible as "sacred," but if God's Word is truly sacred—God-given and worthy of our reverent obedience—we must respect its authority over our lives. Though we are imperfect creatures, prone to self-interest, we must *try* to read God's Word without *any* prejudice, and with a goal of eliminating *any* intellectual dishonesty we detect in ourselves.

Interpreting the Bible is not a matter of picking and choosing, but of exploring and understanding. We study the historical context of each book of the Bible and the culture in which it was written. We grapple with the intentions of the human writers of the text. We try to understand the grammar and syntax of the text in the original language. We treat biblical poetry differently than biblical history. But throughout our exploration of the Scriptures, we acknowledge that the Bible is God's inspired Word, and it has authority over our lives.

The Bible will make us uncomfortable. We won't like everything it says. We will have to wrestle with it and learn how to apply its timeless principles to the times in which we live. But we don't need to read it with a "prejudice of love." If we chip away at the integrity and sufficiency of any portion of God's Word, we undermine everything it says, including the message of salvation, the Good News of Jesus Christ.

God invented love. The Bible is drenched in love. To love as God loves, we must read and apply what is written in its pages; we must read without a political bias or a social agenda. The inerrant Word of God was written by human beings under the inspiration of God and is infallible in its teachings. The entire Bible, every word.

Everything Old Is "New" Again

Long before Rachel Held Evans and other so-called progressive Christians came along, there was Harry Emerson Fosdick.

Born in 1878, Fosdick made a decision at the age of seven to receive Jesus Christ as his Lord and Savior. By the time he was a teenager, Fosdick had decided that he wanted nothing to do with "born-again" evangelical Christianity, though he still wanted to be a Christian. He was concerned about the rise of Christian fundamentalism, and he rejected the doctrines of the Virgin Birth, the inerrancy of Scripture, and the second coming of Christ.

Fosdick went on to study theology at Colgate University under the liberal theologian William Newton Clarke, and he arrived at a set of beliefs based not on Scripture but on his own religious experience. Fosdick became an eloquent speaker and a gifted author whose books sold millions of copies. Ralph Sockman, another prominent New York pastor at the time, called him "the most influential interpreter of religion to his generation."[7] In his writing and speaking, Fosdick concentrated on applying broad Christian principles of love, forgiveness, and peacemaking to everyday problems and relationships.

Harry Emerson Fosdick was extremely successful in popularizing a liberal, unbiblical version of Christianity across America via books, radio broadcasts, and thousands of sermons and lectures. He played a major role in spreading theological liberalism throughout mainline Protestant Christianity. He was a man of seemingly good intentions, who helped to hollow out the church from within.

One faithful Bible teacher who battled Fosdick's eloquent falsehoods and the teachings of other liberal preachers was John Gresham Machen, the last of the great evangelical theologians at Princeton before that institution was consumed by liberalism. Machen, who founded Philadelphia's Westminster Theological Seminary after he was forced out of Princeton, said, "The question is not whether Mr. Fosdick is winning men, but whether the thing to which he is winning them is Christianity."[8]

That is still the question we must ask of the current wave of leaders and teachers who preach a non-evangelical, non-biblical, non-orthodox "Christianity." They are attracting followers; they are winning people to their diluted versions of Christianity. In the process, they claim, they are "saving Christianity," as if the faith that was once for all entrusted to us must be revised in order to be saved from extinction.

Hilary Wakeman, one of the first women ordained as an Anglican priest, wrote a book called *Saving Christianity: New Thinking for Old Beliefs*. What kind of "new thinking" does she advocate for "saving" Christianity? Simply this: She wants to do away with all the "old beliefs." For example, she claims that the doctrine of Christ's divinity "is an assertion that was a product of its time, but one that for some time has actually been contributing to the decline of Christianity."[9] If we are to save Christianity, she writes, "we must have the courage to let it go."

Another doctrine that she believes we must courageously throw overboard is that of the Virgin Birth. Wakeman asserts that the notion of the Virgin Birth "was not important at the time when the gospels and epistles that make up our New Testament were being written," and "it need not be important now."[10]

What does Hilary Wakeman do with the atoning death of Jesus on the cross? She dismisses it entirely.

> Now in the twenty-first century, the concept of
> "Jesus dying for our sins" has become meaningless
> to so many Christians, and offensive to so many
> potential Christians, that it is time to let it become
> one of the optionals.[11]

If the death of Jesus has so little meaning to Wakeman, then what use does she have for the Resurrection? None.

> Rationally we know we can have no proof that Jesus
> made a bodily resurrection after his own death.
> Instead, we are told, we must have faith that he did.[12]

In fact, she compares faith in the literal, historical resurrection of Christ to having faith in "the Emperor's invisible clothes."[13]

Whenever these teachers come along proclaiming a way to "save Christianity," they always claim to have something *new*—for example, Hilary Wakeman's "new thinking for old beliefs" or Brian McLaren's "new kind of Christianity." They think they have invented something new when all they have done is to channel the ghost of Harry Emerson Fosdick.

In 2013, Rachel Held Evans wrote in a CNN blog post, "What millennials really want from the church is not a change in style but a change in substance."[14] But if we change the substance of Christianity, is it still Christianity? Liberals and progressives have a tendency to toss the old truths onto the ash heap and replace them with age-old heresies and a worldly—even Marxist—social gospel. Liberal Christianity inevitably aligns itself with a secular political agenda instead of the Kingdom agenda of Jesus.

In their efforts to "save" Christianity, these progressive leaders have emptied the faith of everything divine and supernatural, leaving us with a Jesus who was born out of wedlock, preached some good sermons, had delusions of grandeur (claiming to be the Son of God), died for no good reason, and is still dead and buried to this day. These leaders have turned their doubts and unbelief into sacraments of an anti-Christian "Christianity." As the apostle Paul warns in 2 Timothy 3:5, these leaders have "a form of godliness" while "denying its power." Paul adds, "Have nothing to do with such people."

It's not our job as Christians to "save" Christianity. It's not our job to change or revise Christianity to make it more palatable to the world. It's not our job to make the gospel of

Jesus Christ more politically correct. We are simply called to believe it, obey it, and proclaim it faithfully.

From One Extreme to the Other

What motivates an evangelical Christian to become a post-evangelical, progressive "Christian"? In many cases, I think their de-conversion from biblical, orthodox Christianity to Bible-doubting, apostate "Christianity" may be the result of a religious overreaction. If you peer into the early years of some progressive "Christians," you may find they came from a background of rigid thinking in which there was no clear dividing line between the essential doctrines of the faith and the peripheral, nonessential doctrines.

There are certain doctrines of the Christian faith that are essential, that are absolute. Reject these and by definition you are not a Christian. As we will see, these core Christian doctrines are summed up in the Apostles' Creed. But apart from those core beliefs, we have great freedom to hold differing views and practice differing faith traditions.

German Protestant theologian Rupertus Meldenius, who lived about a century after Martin Luther, formulated a helpful principle that is rooted in the Scriptures: *In necessariis unitas, in dubiis libertas, in omnibus caritas* (often translated: "in essentials, unity; in nonessentials, liberty; in all things, charity"). One of the great strengths of evangelical Christianity is its ability to unite Christians from many faith traditions around the essential articles of the Christian creed. Unfortunately, many people have grown up in homes and in churches where there was no distinction made between essential and nonessential beliefs. Every doctrine, no matter how minor, was nonnegotiable and absolute, and anyone who disagreed on even the most insignificant point was considered a heretic.

Such black-and-white thinking leads to a very brittle, fragile, all-or-nothing belief system. If some fact or idea happens to upset one little part, the entire system is compromised—"If *that* belief is wrong, what about all my *other* beliefs?"—and everything, essentials and nonessentials alike, come tumbling down like a house of cards. When that happens, people often swing to the opposite extreme. That seems to be the journey that Rachel Held Evans was on, as described in her own words:

> I was a fundamentalist in the sense that I thought salvation means having the right opinions about God and that fighting the good fight of faith requires defending those opinions at all costs. I was a fundamentalist because my security and self-worth and sense of purpose in life were all wrapped up in getting God right—in believing the right things about him, saying the right things about him, and convincing others to embrace the right things about him too. Good Christians, I believed, don't succumb to the shifting sands of culture. Good Christians, I used to think, don't change their minds. . . .
>
> I was a fundamentalist not because of the beliefs I held but because of how I held them: with a death grip.[15]

When she made the decision to trade her fundamentalism for a less dogmatic form of Christianity, she dumped her former beliefs and traditions overboard. "I've wrestled with the evangelical tradition in which I was raised," she writes. "At times I've tried to wring the waters of my first baptism out of my clothes, shake them out of my hair, and ask for a do-over in some other community where they ordain women, vote for Democrats, and believe in evolution."[16]

Like Rachel Held Evans, Brian McLaren made a journey from one extreme to the other. In a 2014 interview on the NPR radio program *On Being*, he said:

I grew up in a little Protestant group called the Plymouth Brethren. . . .

But I kind of reached my turning point as a young fundamentalist. I think I was in seventh grade and my Sunday School teacher said, "You have to choose. You either can believe in God or evolution." And I remember at that age, I thought evolution was absolutely magnificent. . . .

So . . . my first problem was science and my second problem was rock and roll. Those don't fit well with a fundamentalist upbringing. So I was kind of on my way out of this whole thing and then I encountered the Jesus movement in the early seventies and I'm one of those people who had a kind of dramatic conversion through the Jesus movement.[17]

While in his teens, McLaren returned to biblical Christianity. Later, he and his wife started a Bible study group in their home, which grew to become a church that he pastored for twenty-four years. He later wrote, "Like a lot of Protestants, for many years I 'knew' what the gospel was. I 'knew' that the gospel was the message of 'justification by grace through faith.' . . . To my embarrassment, though, about fifteen years ago I stopped knowing a lot of what I previously knew."[18]

It may be instructive to compare the journey of these two postmodern, progressive "Christians," Rachel Held Evans and Brian McLaren, with the journey of two prominent atheists, Dan Barker and Michael Shermer.

Born in 1949, Dan Barker is co-president (with his wife, Annie Laurie Gaylor) of the Freedom From Religion Foundation. He was raised in a conservative Christian family and became a preacher and evangelist at age fifteen. While in high school, he led his Spanish teacher to the Lord. He graduated from Azusa Pacific University with a degree in religion and served as a pastor and a missionary to Mexico. An accomplished musician, he wrote songs and produced music for major Christian record labels. To this day, though he is a prominent atheist, he receives royalty checks for two Christian children's musicals he wrote.

Barker described his mind-set in his autobiography, *Godless: How an Evangelical Preacher Became One of America's Leading Atheists.* A pastor told him of two people in his church who considered the account of Adam and Eve to be a parable rather than a literal historical event. Barker recalled his emotional response:

> I was shocked by this kind of talk. Liberal talk. The fundamentalist mindset does not allow this latitude. To the fundamentalist there is no gray area. Everything is black or white, true or false, right or wrong. . . .
>
> That was the first of many little steps over the next few years. Those initial and timid movements away from fundamentalism were psychologically more traumatic than the intellectual flying leaps that came later. When you are raised to believe that every word in the bible is God-inspired and inerrant, you can't lightly moderate your views on scripture.
>
> I was about 30 years old when I started to have these early questions about Christianity. Not doubts, just questions.[19]

In 1984, after spending nineteen years as a preacher and Christian musician, Dan Barker announced to his friends and family that he had abandoned his faith and had become an atheist. He made a public announcement of his de-conversion on the TV show *AM Chicago*, hosted by Oprah Winfrey. Today, in his leadership position with the Freedom From Religion Foundation, he files lawsuits against any mention of God in the public square, and he engages in public debates with Christians on university campuses.

Michael Shermer is the founder of the Skeptics Society.

He is also editor-in-chief of the society's magazine, *Skeptic*, which seeks to debunk supernatural claims, including religious claims. In his book *How We Believe: Science, Skepticism, and the Search for God*, Shermer tells his story of becoming a Christian:

> In my senior year of high school I accepted Jesus as my savior and became a born-again Christian. I did so at the behest of a close and trusted friend, who assured me this was the road to everlasting life and happiness. . . . At the moment of my conversion, coyotes began howling outside. We took it as a sign that Lucifer was unhappy at the loss of another soul. . . .
>
> With faith in Jesus, I now had eternal life. With faith in God, I was saved. I had found the One True Religion, and it was my duty—indeed it was my pleasure—to tell others about it, including my parents, brothers and sisters, friends, and even total strangers.[20]

He attended church and Christian youth rallies, read his Bible, and prayed. During his sophomore year of college, he read Hal Lindsey's 1970 bestseller, *The Late Great Planet Earth*. The book suggested that the Antichrist would likely appear in the 1970s, and the Rapture of the church would take place in the 1980s. Shermer recalls that he "devoured the book with great credulity."[21] But all was not right with his faith:

There were problems with my conversion from
the beginning however, and I think deep down on
some level I must have known it. First, my motives
for converting, while sincere later, were not quite
as pure at the time—my friend had a sister that
I wanted to get to know better and I figured this
might help. . . . More importantly, there were
chinks in the armor: Another friend at my high
school told me I had chosen the wrong path and
that his faith, Jehovah's Witnesses, was the One True
Religion, making me wonder how another religion
could be as certain it had the truth as my newfound
one did.[22]

Shermer also had many philosophical questions regarding
free will, predestination, and the problem of evil (how can
an all-good, all-powerful God allow evil in the world?). At
Glendale College, he challenged his philosophy professor to
read *The Late Great Planet Earth*, hoping his prof would "see
the light." Instead, the professor typed up a two-page, single-
spaced critique of the book that Shermer has kept ever since.
That critique shattered Shermer's faith and sent him into a
tailspin of doubt. He decided that religion could not answer
his philosophical questions.[23]

In time, Shermer turned his back on his original decision for Christ and proclaimed himself an atheist. Like Dan
Barker, he didn't merely change his private beliefs. He swung
to the opposite pole and became an outspoken missionary for
skepticism and unbelief.

It seems to me there are striking similarities between the paths taken by Dan Barker and Michael Shermer and the paths taken by Rachel Held Evans and Brian McLaren. All four started with rigid beliefs and a black-and-white view of Christianity that allowed no disagreement on any aspect of the faith—essential and nonessential alike. All four ended up abandoning even the essentials of the faith and denying the teachings of the Bible. The difference between the progressive "Christians" and the atheists is one of degree. The atheists toss everything overboard. The progressive "Christians" maintain a form of godliness while denying its power.

We human beings have a hard time finding a biblical balance. We easily swing from pole to pole, from one extreme to the other. I urge you to keep your steps on the narrow path of balance. Hold tightly to the core essentials of the faith, but accept your God-given liberty to question the nonessential issues and change your mind. Respect the same liberty that God grants to your brothers and sisters in Christ.

Above all, in times of doubt and questioning, cling to the promise of the Lord Jesus: "If you hold to my teaching, you are really my disciples. Then you will know the truth, and the truth will set you free."[24] Confess your doubts and questions to the Lord. Promise him that as you work through your questions, you will hold on to all of his teachings. Believe that he *will* reveal his truth to you. If you turn to him, he will not let you fall prey to a false gospel. He will guard your faith and defend your soul against doubt and unbelief.

What Does "Eternal Life" Mean?

Brian McLaren tells the story of how he arrived at a new, post-evangelical definition of the gospel.

> A lunchtime meeting in a Chinese restaurant unconvinced and untaught me. My lunch mate was a well-known Evangelical theologian who quite rudely upset years of theological certainty with one provocative statement: "Most Evangelicals haven't got the foggiest notion of what the gospel really is." He then asked me how I would define the gospel, and I answered . . . by quoting Romans. He followed up with this simple but annoying rhetorical question: "You're quoting Paul. Shouldn't you let Jesus define the gospel? . . . For Jesus, the gospel was very clear: *The kingdom of God is at hand.* . . . Shouldn't you read Paul in light of Jesus, instead of reading Jesus in light of Paul?"[25]

As a result of that conversation, McLaren began to rethink what Jesus meant when he said, "The kingdom of God is at hand." Over time, he came to the conclusion that when Jesus spoke of "the kingdom of God" or "the kingdom of heaven," he was referring to "good news for the poor."[26] McLaren adds, "There is a personal dimension to the kingdom of God, to be sure, in which we have a personal relationship with the King. But there is also a social dimension to the kingdom of God, a dimension that challenges normal human (and religious) assumptions about peace, war, prosperity, poverty, privilege, responsibility, religion, and God."[27]

McLaren likes to surround his views with a haze of uncertainty and vague symbols. "The metaphor is so rich and revolutionary," he claims, "that it resists reduction into a simple definition."[28] But when you boil down his ideas and inspect them carefully, what remains is the same old social gospel, a secular social and political agenda cloaked in religious language—including a rejection of a belief in eternal life in heaven with God. McLaren is simply Harry Emerson Fosdick dressed up in the emperor's new clothes.

If you read McLaren's writings with careful discernment and a clear understanding of the Scriptures, it's easy to hear in his writings echoes from Eden: "Did God really say . . . ?" A mature student of the Bible could readily spot McLaren's errors, but McLaren's unbiblical "gospel" isn't targeted at mature students of the Bible. It is aimed at a generation of biblically unsophisticated young people. McLaren and his fellow progressive "Christians" seem to think they've discovered an entirely new gospel embedded in the words of Jesus—a gospel that generations of theologians and preachers have somehow missed for two thousand years.

McLaren rejects the promise of eternal life in heaven in favor of the idea that Jesus preached a social utopia on earth. He claims that the English translation of the Greek phrase meaning "eternal life" is "misleading."[29] The Greek phrase in question is ζωὴν αἰώνιον (*zōēn aiōnion*). McLaren chooses to translate it "life of the ages."

It's easy to see why McLaren, having rejected the concept

of eternal life, would want to turn Christ's powerful promise into a meaningless word salad like "life of the ages." But whether in Greek or in English, words have meaning, and the meaning of *eternal life* becomes unmistakably clear when you see the phrase used in context (as we will in a moment).

McLaren goes on to say, "A surprisingly large number of committed Christians still assume 'kingdom of God' and 'life of the ages' mean 'life in heaven after you die.' This misbelief is one of the most tragic turns in the history of Christian theology, in my opinion."[30]

But who is being misleading about the Lord's phrase "eternal life"? And who is spreading a tragic misbelief? Let's look at some of Jesus' uses of "eternal life" (which I have italicized below) and you tell me: Is he speaking of a temporal social utopia in this world—as McLaren claims—or is he speaking of living forever in heaven with him?

> "Everyone who has left houses or brothers or sisters or father or mother or wife or children or fields for my sake will receive a hundred times as much and will inherit *eternal life*."[31]

> "Truly I tell you," Jesus replied, "no one who has left home or brothers or sisters or mother or father or children or fields for me and the gospel will fail to receive a hundred times as much in this present age: homes, brothers, sisters, mothers, children and

fields—along with persecutions—and in the age to come *eternal life.*"[32]

"For God so loved the world that he gave his one and only Son, that whoever believes in him shall not perish but have *eternal life.*"[33]

"For my Father's will is that everyone who looks to the Son and believes in him shall have *eternal life,* and I will raise them up at the last day."[34]

"I give them *eternal life,* and they shall never perish; no one will snatch them out of my hand."[35]

"For you granted him authority over all people that he might give *eternal life* to all those you have given him."[36]

In context, when Jesus spoke of eternal life, it is clear he was speaking of our *literally* living forever after death and inheriting a place in heaven in the age to come. And consider this: If the Good News of Jesus Christ was *not* a message of eternal life after death, why did Jesus, as he hung on the cross, tell the believing thief, "Truly I tell you, today you will be with me in paradise"?[37]

Brian McLaren has unfairly caricatured the message of the church this way:

Our contemporary gospel is primarily

INFORMATION ON HOW TO GO TO HEAVEN AFTER YOU DIE

with a large footnote about increasing your personal happiness and success through God

with a small footnote about character development

with a smaller footnote about spiritual experience

with a smaller footnote about social/global transformation.[38]

Are there churches that preach only about how to get to heaven? Are there churches that preach a materialistic "gospel" of success and prosperity? Are there churches that place too little emphasis on developing Christian character or partaking of the deep experience of worship? Are there churches that are not involved in serving widows, orphans, and the poor? I'm sure such churches can be found. But has McLaren fairly characterized the width and depth and breadth of biblical teaching in evangelical churches today? Of course not. His "contemporary gospel" is a straw man and a libel against the church.

In a presentation that McLaren calls "A Tale of Two Gospels," he offers a misleading choice between a "gospel of saving individual souls from hell, and abandoning earth to destruction," and a "gospel of saving earth (including individuals) from human sin, beginning with us."[39] The first, he says, is a gospel of "evacuation," and the second is a gospel of "transformation."[40] Again, he unfairly caricatures the evangelical message to contrast progressive, post-evangelical "Christians" with those cold-hearted, uncaring evangelicals who just can't wait for the end of the world.

McLaren has stacked the deck. There is a third option that he keeps hidden from his readers, and that is the authentic gospel offered in the New Testament. The Good News that Jesus proclaimed in Matthew, Mark, Luke, and John is all-encompassing. It has implications for eternal life *and* our daily lives; for our character development *and* our deep spiritual experience; for individuals *and* for the world.

If you truly want to change the world for the better, stick with what works—the Good News of salvation by grace through faith in Jesus Christ. The authentic gospel message has liberated more oppressed people, unshackled more slaves, elevated the status of more women, brought healing to more sick people, uplifted and empowered more poor people, and founded more hospitals and universities than any other idea or movement in human history. Why are progressives so eager to abandon the only force in history that has ever brought true social and global transformation—that is, the Good News of faith in Jesus Christ?

It amazes me that people who claim to be Christians would take the apostle Paul's warning so lightly:

I am astonished that you are so quickly deserting the one who called you to live in the grace of Christ and are turning to a different gospel—which is really no gospel at all. Evidently some people are throwing you into confusion and are trying to pervert the gospel of Christ. But even if we or an angel from heaven should preach a gospel other than the one we preached to you, let them be under God's curse![41]

The authentic biblical gospel is good news for the poor and the oppressed, as Jesus announces in Luke 4:18 (quoting Isaiah 61:1). But while we are caring for the poor and oppressed; while we seek peace and justice; while we show mercy and forgiveness; while we affirm God's love for all people regardless of race, gender, or class; while we walk humbly with God; while we obey the "one another" commands of Scripture; while we are patient with those who have doubts; while we care for the natural environment God created, we *must* hold fast to the gospel of salvation and eternal life by grace through faith in Jesus Christ. We *must* confess that the Christian gospel does *not* embrace all religions, and that there are *not* many spiritual paths that lead to the same place. We *must* agree with the words of Peter as he stood before the Sanhedrin: "Salvation is found in no one else, for there is no other name under heaven given to mankind by which we must be saved."[42] We *must* agree with Jesus that he is the Way, the Truth, and the Life, and the only way to God the Father.

If *that* is not our gospel, then it is not the gospel of Jesus Christ.

We cannot "save Christianity" by eliminating the Lord's

core teachings about himself and the Kingdom of Heaven. It's not our job to "save Christianity." Jesus saves. We cannot. Our job is to believe, receive, obey, and tell the world.

The *saving* was accomplished the moment Jesus said, "It is finished."

The Extinction of Truth

Poet Thomas Gray once famously observed, "Where ignorance is bliss, 'tis folly to be wise."[1] But history shows that ignorance of the truth can be far from blissful. Here is one tragic case in point.

In an eighteen-month period from 1665 to 1666, an estimated 100,000 people, roughly one-fourth of the population of London, died as a direct result of ignorance.[2] In those days, London was a walled city, with about 400,000 people crowded into an area about twice the size of a Six Flags amusement park. Because the people were unaware of the basic requirements of sanitation, raw sewage flowed down the center of London's cobblestone streets.

The city government kept detailed records of events that

occurred within its walls, including deaths. In February 1665, a single death was recorded in the densely crowded parish of St. Giles-in-the-Fields. The cause of that death was unknown, but the victim exhibited buboes, swelling of the lymph nodes. The people of London took no notice of that one isolated death.

By April, four people had died, all with the same symptoms, yet the official bills of mortality did not list plague as the cause of death. By May, the death toll had reached forty-three—but most of the victims had died in the poorest section of London. City officials were not alarmed. Not yet.

In June, the contagion exploded across the city, and 6,137 people died. The citizens panicked. City officials imposed a brutal quarantine system. In any house where even one person showed symptoms of the plague, officials locked the entire family in the house for forty days, which frequently led to the entire family dying from both disease and hunger.

Officials painted a red cross on the door of a plague house, along with the words *Lord Have Mercy upon Us*. They would post a watchman at the door, armed with a halberd—a pointed spear with a battle-ax attached. As a result, people were terrified of being quarantined and often hid sick family members, which only perpetuated the spread of plague. Instead of containing the disease, the city's well-intentioned actions *increased* the death toll.[3]

Almost as deadly as the plague itself was the ignorance that allowed it to spread. Many people believed that the disease was caused by the stench in the air from filth in the streets. Many Londoners walked about town with nosegays—little flower bouquets—pressed to their faces to ward off the stench and disease. They thought the fragrance of the flowers would protect them from the plague. Some held hands in a circle around a rose bush to breathe in the fragrance—and they would spread the disease through their touch. Some historians believe the old children's rhyme "Ring around the Rosy" refers to superstitious practices used to ward off the plague.

Widespread ignorance helped spread the contagion and inflate the death toll. In July 1665, 17,036 people died. In August, the number of deaths peaked at 31,159.[4] The plague continued to kill Londoners by the hundreds well into 1666.

On September 2, 1666, a fire broke out in the center of the city—a fire that burned for five days and consumed more than 13,000 homes. It became known as the Great Fire of London. The number of deaths in the Great Fire was small, but the blaze killed countless flea-bearing, plague-carrying rats and effectively ended the plague in London.

Though the plague of 1665 and 1666 was largely confined to London, other villages and towns were also affected. One such village was Eyam in Derbyshire, 150 miles north of London. In 1665, a traveler arrived in Eyam with a flea-infested basket of laundry. The fleas spread the plague throughout Eyam.

The church at Eyam was led by a courageous minister named William Mompesson. When many in Eyam panicked and wanted to escape to other villages, Pastor Mompesson urged them to stay in town and pray, lest they spread the plague to neighboring villages. Every Sunday, he would stand on a rock in a dell at the edge of town, preaching outdoors so that members of the congregation would be less likely to infect each other.

By the time the plague had run its course, more than three-quarters of the villagers of Eyam had died—including Pastor Mompesson's own wife. But by calling his parishioners to remain in Eyam instead of fleeing elsewhere, Pastor Mompesson saved countless lives in surrounding towns. His pulpit was nothing but a rock, but he stood firm on that rock and preached the truth.[5]

Today, ignorance of the truth still kills—and spiritual death is spreading like a plague. This dying world needs Christians who will not run in fear but will stand firm on the rock of biblical truth. This world needs Christians who will boldly speak God's truth to a world that is dying from a contagion of lies.

What Is Truth?

In centuries past, our civilization highly valued truth and the certainty that comes from knowing the truth. In the words of Leonardo Da Vinci, "Truth bears the same relation to falsehood as light to darkness; and this truth is in itself so excellent that, even when it dwells on humble and lowly matters, it is still infinitely above uncertainty and lies."[6] He went on to say that those who "live in dreams are better pleased by the . . . reasons and frauds of wits in great and uncertain things, than by those reasons which are certain and natural."[7]

America was founded on the belief that some truths are undeniable and should be recognized by all: "We hold these truths to be self-evident, that all men are created equal, that they are endowed by their Creator with certain unalienable Rights, that among these are Life, Liberty and the pursuit of Happiness."[8] Henry Ward Beecher, the nineteenth-century abolitionist minister, prayed, "Give us that calm certainty of truth, that nearness of thee, that conviction of the reality of the life to come, which we shall need to bear us through the troubles of this [life]."[9]

In our culture today, there is no longer a commonly held love of truth, rationality, and objectivity. As a *Washington Post* columnist declared in 2016, we now live in a "post-truth" world, in which "truth is dead," and "facts are passé."[10]

In place of objective truth and reason, we now have "consensus reality" and a "herd mentality," in which "reality" is what majority opinion says it is. In place of truth and reason, we now have "fake news," in which reality is what biased news sources claim it is. In place of truth and reason, we now have "alternative facts," in which reality is whatever the political establishment claims it to be. In place of truth and reason, we now have political correctness, in which reality is whatever the radical thought-police tell us to think.

We are approaching the cultural madness depicted by George Orwell in his dystopian novel *1984*. In that frightening tale, *truth* is whatever the all-powerful Party says it is. If the Party says two plus two equals five, the people willingly accept it as truth. Whatever Big Brother, the fictive Party leader, *says* is true, even if he said the opposite last week. In the opening chapter of *1984*, the lonely hero of the story stands before the white concrete pyramid of the Ministry of Truth and reads the Party slogan inscribed on the façade: "War Is Peace, Freedom Is Slavery, Ignorance Is Strength."[11]

Why would the so-called Ministry of Truth proclaim such obviously self-contradictory falsehoods on its building? Orwell is telling us that it is possible to construct a society in which lies can be announced as truths—and those lies will become the truths that everyone in society believes. We are seeing Orwell's vision coming to pass in Western society— even in the church.

Visions and Votes

Let's not blame the secular world for the decline of truth in our society. The debasing of truth did not begin in Hollywood, New York, or Washington, DC. It began in the Christian church. For decades, many Christian denominations have abandoned or tried to soft-pedal biblical truth, and our society has followed suit. Take, for example, the story of Marcus Borg.

Born into a Lutheran family in Minnesota, Borg attended Concordia College in Moorhead, Minnesota, which is affiliated with the Evangelical Lutheran Church in America. Though raised in the evangelical Christian faith, Borg was troubled by doubts in his early years. Hoping to settle his doubts, he enrolled at Union Theological Seminary in New York City, a stronghold of liberal theology. He went on to earn degrees at Oxford—a master's in theology and a doctorate in philosophy—before returning to Concordia to teach religion.

In his early thirties, while teaching at Concordia, Borg had a vision while driving across snow-clad rural Minnesota in the wintertime. The sunlight seemed to change to a golden light that (in his words) "suffused everything I saw: the snow-covered fields to left and right, the trees bordering the fields, the yellow and black road signs, the highway itself. Everything glowed."[12] In those moments, he felt the connectedness of everything in the universe. The experience lasted a minute or so, then faded away.

Over the next two years, Borg experienced several more such visions, including two that occurred as he attended orchestra concerts. Then the visions stopped.

Some twenty years later, when Borg was in his fifties, he was flying from Tel Aviv to New York when he had another vision, which seemed to last about forty minutes. He saw everything around him—the airplane, the passengers, the flight attendants, the food on the serving trays, even the fabric of the airliner seats—as luminous, golden, and "filled with glory."[13]

Borg said that these experiences led to his "third conversion"—a conversion to mysticism (his first conversion was to belief in Jesus; his second was to liberal theology). He concluded that these mystical experiences of golden light helped shape his worldview and his beliefs, and they confirmed him in his liberal view of Jesus and the Bible.[14] He became what is now called a "progressive Christian."

As a result of these "conversions," he came to deny the inspiration and authority of Scripture. "I let go of the notion that the Bible is a divine product," he writes. "I learned that it is a human cultural product, the product of two ancient communities, biblical Israel and early Christianity. As such, it contained their understandings and affirmations, not statements coming directly or somewhat directly from God."[15]

Borg also denied claims that Jesus himself made—that he is the Son of God, the Savior of fallen humanity, and the only way to God the Father. "Jesus almost certainly was not born of a virgin, did not think of himself as the Son of God, and did not see his purpose as dying for the sins of the world."[16]

He even denied the central fact on which the Christian faith is founded, the literal and historical resurrection of Jesus Christ from the dead. In a blog post, Borg writes, "I do not think that the gospel stories of Easter require us to think of the resurrection in material physical terms. I see them as parables of the resurrection. Parables are about meaning. They are truth-filled and truthful stories, even as they may not be literally factual."[17]

In 1985, Borg joined a group of 150 liberal theologians and laymen known as the Jesus Seminar. These critics of the Bible started with the assumption that the Bible is untruthful. They took upon themselves the task of separating the "historical" Jesus from the "mythical" Jesus of the four Gospels. How did they decide which parts of the Gospels are true and which are mythical? By voting. They pooled their biases and unbelief, and they sat in collective judgment on the Word of God.

Because the members of the Jesus Seminar were all uniformly liberal in their theology, they wanted to believe in a Jesus who was a social reformer, not a Savior; a Jesus who was neither the son of a virgin nor the Son of God; a Jesus who died but never rose again. From this prejudiced starting point, they evaluated roughly five hundred statements of Jesus recorded in the Gospels. They voted using colored beads. A red bead (worth three points) meant that the statement was, in the voter's mind, probably authentic. A pink bead (worth two points) meant the voter thought Jesus probably said something similar to that statement. A gray bead (worth one point) meant the voter thought a given statement was not a direct quote but probably contained some of Jesus' ideas. A black bead (worth zero points) meant the voter thought that Jesus never said it.[18]

Human folly is fascinating to behold. Some learned and intelligent human beings actually believe they can decide what is real and what is not real by putting the matter to a vote. It makes as much sense as voting on whether the earth is flat or round, whether the law of gravity should be repealed, or whether the War of 1812 really happened. And yet Marcus Borg and his fellow members of the Jesus Seminar—with the broadest of assumptions and the thinnest of evidence—voted to rewrite history and remake Jesus in their own image.

How many statements of Jesus did the Jesus Seminar deem to be reliable? Using their point-scale colored beads, they voted that only thirty-one out of the Lord's five hundred statements were authentic. The rest were considered iffy, strongly doubted, or completely inauthentic—according to their opinion-based vote. Jesus, they concluded, was a mortal man, born of human parents, not a miracle-worker or healer. He did not die for our sins, he did not physically rise from the dead, and the many witnesses who saw him and spoke to him after his death were merely having mystical visions.

And speaking of mystical visions, what about Marcus Borg's own experiences of seeing the people and the world around him transformed by a golden light? I believe Borg's visions actually occurred, but I'm certain they did not come from God. Those visions didn't lead him to a deeper faith in God or a deeper love for God's Word; instead, they drew him further into error and away from the biblical faith he had already abandoned.

Where would a seductive, deceptive golden light come from? Consider this: Satan's name in Latin is Lucifer, which literally means "light-bringer." The apostle Paul describes Satan as an "angel of light" who has duped many so-called "Christians" into doing his bidding:

> Such people are false apostles, deceitful workers, masquerading as apostles of Christ. And no wonder, for Satan himself masquerades as an angel of light. It is not surprising, then, if his servants also masquerade as servants of righteousness. Their end will be what their actions deserve.[19]

Marcus Borg died in 2015. Through his writings, however, he continues to exert an influence over what has come to be known as "progressive Christianity" or the "emerging church" movement or the "post-evangelical" movement.

Borg has been acclaimed as a mentor and role model by many leaders of the "progressive Christian" movement.

Whereas biblical, evangelical Christianity emphasizes the authority of the Bible, the forgiveness of sin, the atoning death of Jesus on the cross, and eternal life by grace through faith in Jesus alone, "progressive Christianity" rejects these doctrines. This mutated form of Christianity cherry-picks the Bible and the words of Jesus, claims that all religions lead to the same God, and seeks to build a utopian "kingdom of heaven" on earth through a liberal-progressive social and political agenda. Leaders of this movement, many of whom claim to be evangelicals, say that truth is unattainable and that certainty should be condemned as a lack of faith.

If we in the church were defending the truth and proclaiming it as we should, we could arrest the decline of truth in our society. Jesus called us to be salt and light.[20] Salt preserves and light illuminates. If our culture is sinking into corruption and darkness, it's because we are not doing the job that Jesus called us to do.

In John 18, Jesus tells Pontius Pilate, "The reason I was born and came into the world is to testify to the truth. Everyone on the side of truth listens to me."[21] Pilate replies with a question: "What is truth?"[22]

Apparently, Jesus saw a dismissive attitude in that question, so he left it unanswered. But to his disciples, who honestly hungered for the truth, Jesus affirmed again and again what the truth is and why truth is so important. Our understanding of truth shapes our thinking, our beliefs, our actions, and our relationships.

Tragically, many supposedly Christian speakers and authors now respond to Jesus and the Bible just as Pilate did: "What is truth?"

The Truth about "True Humility"

Who are these speakers, authors, and leaders I'm talking about? They come under a variety of labels: emerging (or emergent) church, post-Protestants, post-evangelicals, liberals, post-liberals, progressives, post-charismatics, postmoderns, and more. One of the leaders in this movement, Brian McLaren, writes:

> I drive my car and listen to the Christian radio station, something my wife always tells me I should stop doing ("because it only gets you upset"). There I hear preacher after preacher be so absolutely sure of his bombproof answers and his foolproof *biblical* interpretations. . . . And the more sure he seems, the less I find myself wanting to be a Christian, because on this side of the microphone, antennas, and speaker, life isn't that simple, answers aren't that clear, and nothing is that sure.[23]

Among postmodern "Christians," the only certain truth is that there is no certainty. They tell us it's a virtue to doubt every teaching of Scripture and a sin to be certain of the gospel and claims of Christ. They tell us that being confident that the Bible says what it means and means what it says is arrogance. True humility, they say, is to be vague about what we believe. More than a century ago, G. K. Chesterton observed this same upside-down, inside-out definition of humility in the apostate Christianity of his day. In his 1908 book *Orthodoxy*, he writes:

> What we suffer from to-day is humility in the wrong place. . . . A man was meant to be doubtful about himself, but undoubting about the truth; this has been exactly reversed. Nowadays the part of a man that a man does assert is exactly the part he ought not to assert—himself. The part he doubts is exactly the part he ought not to doubt—the Divine Reason.[24]

The misplaced, misdefined notion of humility promoted by progressive "Christians" today is exactly what Chesterton described in 1908. The "progressives" doubt God, his Word, and his Son—but they don't have any doubts whatsoever about the progressive sexual agenda or social agenda or political agenda. They question the Bible while making certainties and sacraments out of gender politics, victim politics, environmental politics, and on and on. Subordinating the gospel to the political agendas of this fallen world is not an act of humility. It is breathtaking arrogance.

Brian McLaren expresses the false humility of progressive "Christianity" in *A Generous Orthodoxy*:

> We must . . . never underestimate our power to be wrong when talking about God, when thinking

about God, when imagining God. . . . A generous orthodoxy, in contrast to the tense, narrow, controlling, or critical orthodoxies of so much of Christian history, doesn't take itself too seriously. It is humble; it doesn't claim too much; it admits it walks with a limp.[25]

God never intended that the church should walk with a limp. His truth gives us the strength to run with confidence. That is why the Scriptures tell us, "Stand firm then, with the belt of truth buckled around your waist, with the breastplate of righteousness in place, and with your feet fitted with the readiness that comes from the gospel of peace."[26] Yet the misguided notion that uncertainty equals humility is rampant throughout the progressive, postmodern camp. Rachel Held Evans writes, "My interpretation can only be as inerrant as I am, and that's good to keep in mind."[27] That sounds like a reasonable statement, and even a genuinely humble statement. It would be, if she applied it in such peripheral doctrinal matters as mode of baptism or speculation about the end times. But when we apply this notion of humility to the absolutes of the Christian faith, it becomes a statement of arrogance and a rejection of the authority of Scripture.

There are certain core truths in the Bible that are not subject to various interpretations. Jesus has told us that he is the way, the truth, and the life, and the only way to God the Father. He has told us, "Enter through the narrow gate. For wide is the gate and broad is the road that leads to destruction, and many enter through it. But small is the gate and narrow the road that leads to life, and only a few find it."[28] He has not left us any wiggle room for "interpreting" his words and finding some hidden meaning there.

Jesus holds us accountable for what the Bible plainly, unambiguously says. Again and again in the Gospels, Jesus says, "Have you not read what God said to you . . . ?" "Is it not written . . . ?" "Have you not read in the Book of Moses . . . ?" "Is it not written in your Law . . . ?"[29] He will not let us get away with the progressive, postmodern dodge that we are "too humble" to interpret and proclaim God's Word.

On most issues, the Bible speaks with such obvious clarity that we can only "reinterpret it" by twisting it beyond recognition. It's a slander against God and his Word to claim that the Bible is so murky and unclear that we must, "in all humility," conclude that we don't really know what it says.

Genuine Christian humility begins when we submit ourselves in awe and reverence before God and his Word. *Genuine* Christian humility begins when we accept the gospel of Jesus Christ as truth. *Genuine* Christian humility begins when we accept with certainty and faith the truth of the cross of Christ. Martyn Lloyd-Jones put it this way:

> Do you know what the gospel does? What the cross does? It shows you to yourself. And nothing else in the whole world does that but the cross. There is nothing that will ever humble a man or a nation but the cross of Christ. . . . The cross tells us the simple plain truth about ourselves. . . .

When I look at that cross and see him dying
there, what he tells me is this: you have nothing
whereof to boast. The cross tells me that I am a
complete failure, and that I am such a failure that
he had to come from heaven, not merely to teach
and preach in this world, but to die on that cross.
Nothing else could save us.[30]

Genuine Christian humility does not begin with doubt.
It begins with acceptance of the truth about ourselves and
the truth about Jesus our Lord. It begins with the gospel and
the cross of Christ.

Targeting the Young

The most insidious aspect of today's post-evangelical, postmodern "Christianity" is that it targets the young. The target
demographic for this movement appears to be eighteen- to
thirty-year-olds. Young people are looking for significance and
an identity, a sense that they are engaged in something important. Eager to change the world, they may be easily swayed
by slogans and arguments that sound plausible but don't hold
water. Fired up with a message that seems dynamic and righteous, they may be especially attracted to the progressive, post-
evangelical social gospel. I'm convinced that this movement is
part of a satanic strategy to seduce an entire generation and
inoculate their minds against the truth of the gospel.

The leaders of the postmodern, progressive, emerging
church like to call their agenda "a conversation" instead of

a movement. In a 2014 blog post, Brian McLaren laid out "key next steps" for the emergent conversation, including "the creation of a national, trans-denominational campus ministry . . . and the development of a new genre of progressive Christian worship music."[31] Clearly, he has young people in his sights.

What are the themes that dominate this "conversation"? McLaren says,

> Beneath the surface, influence continues to expand, especially among young Evangelicals and those uncomfortable with the marriage between American Evangelicalism and the Religious Right. Along with LGBT equality, surprising numbers of Evangelicals are quietly but consistently moving towards greater concern for the full equality for women, the environment, racial and interfaith reconciliation, the elimination of torture, peacemaking, poverty reduction, and related issues."[32]

In short, the agenda of the postmodern "Christians" is nearly identical to the political and social agenda of the secular left.

McLaren goes on to say that postmodern "Christians" like himself are "eager to engage with questions that have been suppressed—including rethinking penal substitutionary atonement theory, biblical inerrancy and interpretation, and the violence of God."[33] He would have us believe there is some sinister evangelical cabal that is "suppressing" questions about atonement, the reliability of Scripture, and violence in Old Testament when, in fact, these questions are openly, frankly discussed in evangelical churches, universities, and seminaries every day.

We need to be clear about what McLaren is saying here. "Rethinking" the doctrine of substitutionary atonement is code for denying what the Scriptures teach about the meaning of the death of Jesus Christ. "Rethinking" biblical inerrancy and interpretation means denying the truthfulness and reliability of God's Word. "Rethinking" the "violence of God" means libeling the God depicted in Old Testament accounts of the Flood and God's judgments against idolatrous, human-sacrificing Canaanite tribes. "Rethinking" means cherry-picking what we like in the Bible and suppressing what we find unpalatable.

Many Christians in evangelical churches now embrace universalism, the notion that God will ultimately save everyone—that is, no one goes to hell. People who profess to be Christians while preaching that all religions lead to heaven are a menace to the church. Our greatest struggle is not with atheists, but with "Christians" inside the church who deny that Jesus is God and that he is the only way to the Father.

These false teachers are leading a generation away from faith in Jesus Christ and into a wasteland of uncertainty and unbelief. The questions they ask are various forms of the same question the serpent posed to Eve in Genesis 3:1: "Did God really say . . . ?" The satanic strategy has not changed since the beginning of history. It starts with a conversation, a question—not a blunt assault on God's truth, but a sly note of doubt about God's words and God's character. Postmodern "Christians" are planting these same sly questions and doubts in the souls of the next generation.

If you are a parent, grandparent, pastor, youth leader, teacher, or just a committed, biblical Christian who loves God's truth, you need to know the lies that are being spread within the evangelical church. And you need to know how to combat those lies with biblical truth and certainty.

4

The Post-Truth Church in a Post-Christian World

The beautiful, historic Church of the Good Shepherd had stood at 79 Conklin Avenue in Binghamton, New York, since 1879. But in 2010, the Episcopal Diocese of Central New York sold the building to a Muslim imam, who converted it into a mosque called the Islamic Awareness Center. The cross atop the church was torn down, and the beautiful stained-glass windows were defaced. A church that had faithfully preached Christ for more than 130 years was silenced by its own diocese.

One might assume that the church had been in decline, but at the time of the sale it was thriving and growing and actively serving the community. In fact, the congregation had offered to buy the church building from the diocese for more than $150,000, but instead the diocese shut the church down and sold it to the Muslim group for a mere $50,000. Why?

Therein lies a story—a tale of the vindictiveness and intolerance of liberal "Christianity."

Eight years earlier, the Church of the Good Shepherd had been a dying and dwindling congregation. Then the Reverend Matt Kennedy and his wife, Anne, arrived to begin their ministry. Rev. Kennedy was an orthodox Anglican minister who held firmly to "the faith that was once for all entrusted to God's holy people."[1] He preached a biblical gospel. From his pulpit, he fed the spiritually hungry, and at the church's soup kitchen and neighborhood block parties, he fed the physically hungry. Weekly Bible studies drew many university students. The once-aging demographic of the church began trending younger under Kennedy's leadership.

His uncompromising preaching of the Word, combined with genuine compassion for the poor, caused the congregation to grow rapidly. In a few short years, the church helped to transform the surrounding neighborhood. At the same time, Rev. Kennedy struggled inwardly over the Episcopal Church's departure from biblical orthodoxy, including its decision to confirm openly gay bishops.

As the denomination moved further away from biblical orthodoxy, the Church of the Good Shepherd joined with other orthodox churches to form the Anglican Communion Network. These congregations wanted to remain with the Episcopal Church while working and praying that the leaders and bishops of the denomination would repent. Rev. Kennedy also wrote blog posts for an orthodox Anglican website. However, his efforts to persuade the Episcopal Church to obey its own Scriptures merely provoked the liberal powers-that-be in the diocese.

In 2003, Rev. Kennedy had a conversation with the bishop of the diocese, who days earlier had voted to confirm openly gay bishops. Kennedy recalled, "I told our bishop we would prefer for him not to come and preach at our church or to celebrate Communion. . . . I asked him how he could possibly vote the way he did, and he said, 'Well, I mean I prayed about it, and I just really felt the Holy Spirit leading me to do that.' I said, 'Well, you know the texts I'm going to show you—Romans 1 and 1 Corinthians 6:9.' He said, 'Yes, I know those texts, but the Jesus I know in my heart wouldn't have inspired those to be written.'"[2]

What a shocking statement! How does a church leader dare to pass judgment on God's Word? How do liberal "Christians" have the nerve to reject Scripture for not conforming to current notions of "political correctness"? Rev. Kennedy explains it this way: "There's a mentality among most bishops in the Episcopal Church . . . [that] 'The Bible represents God's Word to people in the past and we are God's people in the present. That's just their understanding of him, and we have our own understanding of him, and the Spirit's going to lead us in new ways.'"[3] By that line of reasoning, it's no problem to cross out any passage of Scripture that makes us uncomfortable. Why wrestle with Scripture when you can simply say, "The Jesus I know in my heart wouldn't have inspired that"?

For three years, the local church continued to thrive, and Rev. Kennedy prayed that the denomination and the diocese would return to biblical orthodoxy. But instead they continued their wayward, leftward drift. Kennedy met with the officers of his parish, and they agreed unanimously that the Church of the Good Shepherd could no longer go down the path the Episcopal Church was traveling. They needed to part ways.

But there was a problem. In 1979, the Episcopal Church had adopted the "Dennis Canon," which established that all parish property would be held in trust by the diocese, and any church that attempted to leave the denomination would have its "real and personal property"—including real estate, furnishings, and bank accounts—seized by the diocese. Understanding the ramifications of the Dennis Canon, the Church of the Good Shepherd made an offer to buy the church property in 2007, prior to separating from the denomination.

The bishop seemed agreeable, but told Rev. Kennedy, "You can't make an offer to buy the property yet . . . because you're still *part* of the Episcopal Church. You have to wait until you *leave* the Episcopal Church, then you can make the offer."[4]

Rev. Kennedy recalled, "I was a little bit worried about that, because, once you leave, legally . . . if they want to apply the Dennis Canon, they're not *bound* to make any agreement with us. They could just take the property."[5] But Kennedy and the vestry officials took the bishop at his word, believing that their leaving would simply be the beginning of a negotiation over price.

After the separation was complete, Reverend Kennedy

contacted the bishop to open the negotiations. However, he said, "just as I'd feared, immediately the tone changed with the bishop and the office in central New York."[6]

The diocese rejected the church's first offer, which was $150,000 for just the church building, with the possibility of additional payment later to cover the rectory, where the Kennedys were living. When Rev. Kennedy asked for a counteroffer, the diocese wouldn't give one. When the church made another offer, one that was more generous, the diocese replied with "another flat *no*."[7]

Next, Rev. Kennedy and two church wardens went to Syracuse for a face-to-face meeting with the bishop and an attorney, but there was no negotiation. Instead, they were told they had six weeks to vacate the church premises and leave behind all the church's assets.

The church had insurance coverage that enabled them to fight the eviction in court for two years, but the court ultimately sided with the diocese. The church quickly arranged to hold its next service in the gymnasium of the Conklin Avenue First Baptist Church.

The Kennedys could no longer live in the parsonage, so they began packing up their belongings to move to an apartment. While they were packing, a Roman Catholic priest called. Two Catholic parishes were being merged into one, leaving the nearby St. Andrews Catholic Church property vacant and for sale. It had a rectory on the property, a large school building, and a parking lot. Rev. Kennedy could immediately move his family into the rectory.

"We were so thankful," he recalled. "It was such a gracious

thing. It was amazing how God works the timing out. They [St. Andrews] had just left a month before we moved in. So it was amazing timing." Eventually, Church of the Good Shepherd was able to purchase the St. Andrews building and grounds, and that's where they meet to this day.[8]

The story ended happily for the Church of the Good Shepherd, for its minister and its people. But you have to wonder what was in the hearts of the leaders of the diocese. They could have allowed the congregation to continue worshiping in its historic and beautiful building—and the church was prepared to pay full market value. But the Episcopal leaders chose to sell the property at a loss, to see the church desecrated and turned into a mosque, just to punish those believers for upholding the Word of Truth.

Liberal, progressive "Christianity" claims to be compassionate and moral, but these actions seem vindictive and un-Christian.

A Progressive "Christian" and Moral Relativist

Tony Jones is a longtime leader in the emerging-church movement and progressive "Christianity." From 2005 to 2008, Jones was national coordinator of Emergent Village, an organization that popularized the emerging church ideology. He has also served as theologian-in-residence at Solomon's Porch in Minneapolis, pastored by Jones's business partner, Doug Pagitt, another leading figure in the emerging-church movement.

Jones has openly declared his praise for moral relativism[9] and his support for LGBTQ rights and same-sex marriage (he has officiated at least one gay marriage ceremony). In one blog post, Jones praised a gay atheist sex-advice columnist as possibly "America's premier sex ethicist."[10]

Jones cites the columnist's assertion that, while monogamy is the right choice for many couples, there are people who need more than one sex partner. Such a view of marriage relationships, Jones adds, "will immediately irk most Christians. Christianity has traditionally—although not unequivocally—held to a strict standard of monogamy. At least in theory. In practice, Christian men have, over the last two millennia, had the opportunity for sexual dalliances through mistresses, concubines, and prostitutes. Of course, there were puritanical moments in history, but the American moment was a particularly puritanical [one]."[11]

Not true. Christianity, as taught by Christ himself and embodied in the entire New Testament, has always upheld a monogamous view. Jesus, truly the greatest sex ethicist in history, said, "I tell you that anyone who looks at a woman lustfully has already committed adultery with her in his heart."[12] When God instituted marriage, he declared, "That is why a man leaves his father and mother and is united to his wife, and they become one flesh."[13] And the New Testament writer to the Hebrews said, "Marriage should be honored by all, and the marriage bed kept pure, for God will judge the adulterer and all the sexually immoral."[14]

If Tony Jones is a theologian, as he claims, then these Scripture passages are surely familiar to him. He must be aware that biblical Christianity always condemns adultery in all its forms, from lust to polyamory. Whenever "Christian men" have engaged in "sexual dalliances through mistresses, concubines, and prostitutes," they have done so in violation of the teachings of Christ and Christianity. The notion that the church has ever accepted sexual sin as normal is simply and dangerously wrong.

Jones writes that the atheist columnist's sexual ethic "is primarily one of realism: human beings are animals who, until very recently, procreated like animals. It is evolutionarily dishonest to demand monogamy of a species predisposed against it. It's not impossible to be monogamous, he says, but it is super difficult."[15]

Jones adds, "I don't know if [the columnist's] ethic jibes with a biblical, Christian view of sexuality. But I do know . . . [he's] more realistic about sex than most Christians I've talked to about sex. . . . I also know that, for the first time in my life I've met Christians who are in 'open' marriages or are practicing polyamory—and I'm committed that my theological/ethical response to them be both Christian and pragmatic/realistic."[16]

These are the thoughts of one of the leading authors and speakers in the emerging-church movement, a teacher who has taught theology at Fuller Theological Seminary. Jones continues to wield great influence in the progressive "Christian" world as a self-proclaimed moral relativist. How can anyone who so utterly rejects the authority of Scripture teach the Scriptures and theology?

In a church where the authority of Scripture is respected, the teaching of moral relativism would not be tolerated. The toleration of sin that Tony Jones displays in his speaking and writing is the same toleration of sin the apostle Paul confronts in 1 Corinthians 5. Not only were the Corinthians tolerant of sin, but they were *proud* of their tolerance. They boasted of it.

God expects Christians today to uphold the same standards of chastity and moral purity that Paul demanded of the Christians in Corinth. Paul's prescription for dealing with a flagrant, openly accepted case of incestuous adultery in Corinth sounds harsh to twenty-first-century ears: "Expel the wicked person from among you."[17] But it was truly an act of love toward the sinner: "Hand this man over to Satan for the destruction of the flesh, so that his spirit may be saved on the day of the Lord."[18]

As proof of the fact that Paul's command to "expel" the sinner from church was motivated by love, turn to 2 Corinthians 2:6-8 and see the result of that expulsion: "The punishment inflicted on him by the majority is sufficient. Now instead, you ought to forgive and comfort him, so that he will not be overwhelmed by excessive sorrow. I urge you, therefore, to reaffirm your love for him." The tough love of church discipline restored the man to moral sanity and to fellowship in the church.

Spiritual defection begins when we give an atheist sex columnist greater moral authority than the Word of God. It begins when we ignore individual verses of Scripture that get in our way. In time, we decide that entire books of the Bible are troubling: "Maybe Paul didn't really write Colossians—that doesn't sound like something he would say."

Then we decide that Paul must have misinterpreted Jesus, so let's ignore *all* of Paul's letters. Let's be "red-letter Christians" and pay attention only to the words of Jesus, the words some Bibles emphasize in red ink.

But wait! Some of the red-letter passages pose problems as well. Some of what Jesus says sounds narrow-minded and intolerant. "Well, how do we know Jesus really said that? The Jesus I know in my heart would never have said such-and-such."

On and on it goes, chopping up Scripture according to our biases and prejudices, everyone believing what is right in his or her own mind. Where does it end?

It ends, of course, in disobedience and unbelief. That's why the Scriptures warn, "Do not add to what I command you and do not subtract from it, but keep the commands of the LORD your God that I give you."[19] Instead of editing out the difficult portions of God's Word, we must wrestle honestly with Scripture, understand it thoroughly, and obey it in true humility.

Post-Truth "Christians" in a Post-Christian World

In Psalm 11:3, David asks, "When the foundations are being destroyed, what can the righteous do?" Today, we are seeing the foundations of Christianity being destroyed by people who claim to be Christians.

There is a subtle deception that underlies—and ultimately undermines—progressive "Christianity." Postmodern "Christians" claim that, in order to reach the postmodern generation, we must speak their language. So far, so good. To reach any culture with the gospel—an African culture, an Asian culture, or the postmodern culture—we must translate the Good News into the language of that culture. But in the process of translating the Good News, the progressives have changed and corrupted it. They have destroyed the foundations. Instead of calling our dying culture to repentance and faith, they have accommodated their "Christian" faith to the dying culture. They have eliminated the very truths that make Christianity Christian.

Retired Episcopal bishop John Shelby Spong was one of the leading post-truth dismantlers of the foundations of Christianity. He wrote a series of books criticizing the Bible and promoting a new kind of "Christianity"—one without sin or guilt. In an interview, Spong said, "This self-denigration stuff—Jesus died for my sins—is nothing but a guilt message. That's the thing we've got to get out from under. That's not Christianity."[20]

Bishop Spong's new kind of "Christianity" is a religion even an atheist can love. In *The God Delusion*, Richard Dawkins, the chief spokesman for atheism today, writes, "Bishop John Shelby Spong . . . is a nice example of a liberal bishop whose beliefs are so advanced as to be almost unrecognizable to the majority of those who call themselves Christians."[21]

As you look at progressive "Christianity," as you read the writings of its proponents and see it in action, it becomes clear that many progressive "Christians" have a passion and a longing to be accepted and approved by our postmodern, post-Christian culture. They have given the old Harry Emerson Fosdick liberalism a new coat of paint. As a result, unbelievers and the secular left are saying, "We love this kind of Christianity! We love this kind of ambiguity and doubt and uncertainty."

An example of the approval progressive "Christianity" is winning from the secular left was published in the left-leaning *Daily Beast*. The headline read, "They Have Faith Their Church Will Change." Journalist Brandon Withrow writes:

> They're young, liberal, LGBTQ+, pro-choice, feminist, science loving, climate change accepting, and immigrant welcoming. They're evangelicals.
>
> No, this is not a report from an alternate universe, where history took a different turn. This is about a growing rift in the evangelical continuum. . . .
>
> It's an internal divide that's forced some progressive evangelicals to part ways with the name. Just this week, co-founder of the progressive Red Letter Christian movement, Tony Campolo, told *Premier* that "a lot of people who are evangelical in

their theology do not want to be called 'evangelicals' anymore." Being evangelical in the United States means "you're anti-gay, you're anti-women, you're pro-war."[22]

Withrow notes, however, that some progressive "Christians" want to keep the label "evangelical" but change what it means:

> "Almost nothing could push me to give up the word 'evangelical'," insists the 24-year old Brandan Robertson, a progressive, bisexual Christian activist. . . . "It really embodies the core of my spirituality—I am a person of good news." . . .
> He's "somewhere in the middle" of the pro-life/pro-choice debate. He longs for the end of "gender binaries" and patriarchy. . . . He's spoken at the White House Summit on Bullying, been interviewed on NPR, and has bylines in *TIME*, the *Washington Post*, and Religion News Service.[23]

If you abandon the foundation of Christianity—the Scriptures and the atoning death and resurrection of Christ—and replace the Christian gospel with the secular left agenda of Darwinism, climate change, identity politics, victim oppression politics, LGBTQ politics, and on and on, you will become the darling of the media and the leftist political establishment. You'll be interviewed on CNN, MSNBC, and NPR, and you'll write for the *Washington Post* and *New York Times*, and you'll be praised by the *Daily Beast* and *Huffington Post*. You can call yourself a "person of good news," but it won't be the Good News of salvation by grace through faith in Christ.

Jesus said, "If you hold to my teaching, you are really my disciples. Then you will know the truth, and the truth will set you free."[24] The progressive "Christians," by their own admission, do not hold to the Lord's teaching—yet they still want to be seen as his disciples. Jesus said we can't have it both ways. His truth will set us free. Rejecting, revising, altering, editing, or ignoring his truth leads to slavery.

If Satan wants one thing for us, it's to keep us in a condition of slavery. He wants us to be bound in chains of doubt, ambiguity, uncertainty, confusion, and delusion. Yet these progressive "Christians" directly contradict Jesus' own words and speak of uncertainty and confusion as if it were freedom.

In the early years of their ministry, emerging-church leaders Rob Bell and his wife, Kristen, were interviewed by Andy Crouch for a cover story in *Christianity Today*. Describing progressive "Christianity," Rob Bell said, "This is not just the same old message with new methods."[25] In other words, this new "Christianity" was radically different from biblical Christianity. He was questioning old beliefs about the Bible and "discovering the Bible as a human product. . . . The Bible is still in the center for us, but it's a different kind of center. We want to embrace mystery, rather than conquer it."[26]

Kristen Bell added, "Life in the church had become so small. It had worked for me for a long time. Then it stopped working. . . . I grew up thinking that we've figured out the

Bible, that we knew what it means. Now I have no idea what most of it means. And yet I feel like life is big again—like life used to be black and white, and now it's in color."[27]

Like most progressive "Christians," Rob and Kristen Bell rarely express their view of the Bible in clear, concrete terms. Where the Bible speaks with clarity and certainty, they speak in metaphors and mysteries. Trying to pin them down is like trying to nail Jell-O to the wall. But when you boil it all down, you're left with the same old liberal social gospel, the same secular-left political/social agenda.

Saying that life used to be black and white and now it's in color is not the kind of freedom Jesus was talking about. There are many truths in life that are completely black and white—the laws of gravity, the laws of thermodynamics, the speed of light, the axioms of mathematics. Jesus tells us that his teachings are in that same category of black-and-white truth, and if we hold to his teachings, we will know the truth and will truly be free.

Jesus warned, "Watch out for false prophets. They come to you in sheep's clothing, but inwardly they are ferocious wolves. By their fruit you will recognize them. Do people pick grapes from thornbushes, or figs from thistles? Likewise, every good tree bears good fruit, but a bad tree bears bad fruit."[28] Satan's strategy is to infiltrate the church with wolves who look like sheep, talk like sheep, act like sheep, dress like sheep—but once they are inside the fold with the sheep, they revert to their wolfish ways. Apostasy is always an inside job.

Judas Iscariot was a member of the Lord's inner circle—one of the twelve original disciples—yet he was a wolf in sheep's clothing. He had the light of Christ but had never received the life of Christ. He had tasted the truth but had never feasted on it. Many churches that call themselves evangelical are full of people who have tasted the truth but have never internalized it. The presence of such people in the church creates confusion, destruction, and apostasy in the church.

Not every churchgoer, pastor, author, or speaker in the church is an authentic believer in the truth of the gospel. Some are wolves in sheep's clothing. I can't judge the heart of any person. I can't judge anyone else's faith or motives. But Jesus calls us to judge the fruit of their lives, the fruit of their words and deeds: "By their fruit you will recognize them."

By the time Jude wrote his brief New Testament epistle, the wolves in sheep's clothing that Jesus had warned about were already evident in the church. "Certain individuals whose condemnation was written about long ago have secretly slipped in among you," Jude writes. "They are ungodly people, who pervert the grace of our God into a license for immorality and deny Jesus Christ our only Sovereign and Lord."[29]

That is why Jude urges his readers to "contend for the faith that was once for all entrusted to God's holy people."[30]

Notice that Jude doesn't merely say, "Contend for faith." He's not talking about just any old faith. Rather he says, "Contend for *the* faith."

On its own, faith is merely the act of believing. But *the* faith is the body of biblical truth taught by Jesus, handed down to us by his apostles, the foundation of what we believe.

The faith is God's revelation of himself in Scripture. *The* faith is the truth that Jesus alone is the Way, the Truth, and the Life. *The* faith is obedience to the authority of God's Word. *The* faith is the certainty that the Bible is a closed book—it cannot be added to or subtracted from. We are custodians and stewards of *the* faith. Do you feel the weight of that responsibility?

Several years ago, I was called to serve as the trustee of the last will and testament of a wealthy business leader. That responsibility caused me about three years of heartburn and sleepless nights because several family members contested the will. I told them, "I am responsible to carry out the last wishes of the one who entrusted this responsibility to me."

God has entrusted something to us that is infinitely more valuable than an earthly estate. He has entrusted *the faith* to us. He has entrusted the gospel of Jesus Christ to us, and he is watching to see whether we will prove worthy of that trust. As custodians and stewards of the truth of God's Word, we are responsible to pass the gospel along to the next generation. It's a weighty responsibility. Are we worthy of the trust God has placed in us? Are we committed to safeguarding his truth and contending for the faith?

In a post-Christian, post-truth world, it's a faith we can be sure of. It's the truth that sets us free.

How Biblical Truth Has Shaped History

It seems that Bible-believing Christians have become the true villains of history.

In *Everything Must Change*, Brian McLaren decries "the dark side of the Christian religion's track record . . . the Crusades, witch burnings, colonialism, slavery, the Holocaust, apartheid, environmental irresponsibility, mistreatment of women."[1]

McLaren claims young people are fleeing the church because "the Christian religion appears to be a failed religion. . . . It has specialized in people's destination in the afterlife but has failed to address significant social injustices in this life. It has focused on 'me' and 'my soul' and 'my spiritual life' and 'my eternal destiny,' but it has failed to address the dominant societal and global realities of their lifetime: systemic injustice, systemic poverty, systemic ecological crisis, systemic dysfunctions of many kinds."[2]

Is McLaren's condemnation of Christianity's track record true? Is it a fair criticism? No. McLaren and his fellow progressive "Christians" operate from a misunderstanding of history and a misunderstanding of the Bible. They also misstate the nature of their own progressive "Christian" agenda—an agenda based not on biblical principles, but on the agenda of the secular left.

The worst accusation McLaren lays at the doorstep of the church is the Nazi Holocaust. "After all," McLaren writes, "Hitler was a Catholic in good standing, and Germany was ostensibly a Christian country dually resourced by Roman Catholicism and the Reformation heritage of Martin Luther, both of which contributed significantly to the anti-Semitism that energized Nazism."[3]

The "Hitler was a Christian" canard has circulated in atheist circles for decades. Adolf Hitler did claim to be a Christian in some public speeches, but in truth he detested Christianity. Though raised in a Catholic home, Hitler revealed through a series of private "table talk" conversations (which were transcribed by a stenographer during the war years) that he viewed Christianity as a "rotten branch" that "falls of itself."[4] In a conversation on December 13, 1941, with several of his top advisors, including Nazi foreign minister Joachim von Ribbentrop and propaganda minister Joseph Goebbels, Hitler said,

The war will be over one day. I shall then consider that my life's final task will be to solve the religious problem. Only then will the life of the German native be guaranteed once and for all.

I don't interfere in matters of belief. Therefore I can't allow churchmen to interfere with temporal matters. The organized lie must be smashed. The state must remain the absolute master. . . .

After all, it was only between the sixth and eighth centuries that Christianity was imposed on our peoples by princes who had an alliance of interests with the shavelings [a disparaging reference to tonsured priests]. Our peoples had previously succeeded in living all right without this religion. . . .

When all is said, we have no reason to wish that the Italians and Spaniards should free themselves from the drug of Christianity. Let's be the only people who are immunized against the disease.[5]

Joseph Goebbels, in his wartime diaries, noted that "the Führer is deeply religious, though completely anti-Christian. He views Christianity as a symptom of decay. Rightly so. It is a branch of the Jewish race."[6]

Historian Alan Bullock, in *Hitler: A Study in Tyranny*, writes, "In Hitler's eyes, Christianity was a religion fit only for slaves; he detested its ethics in particular. Its teaching, he declared, was a rebellion against the natural law of selection by struggle and the survival of the fittest. . . . Once the war was over, he promised himself, he would root out and destroy the influence of the Christian Churches, but until then he would be circumspect."[7]

The Holocaust was not inspired by anything in the Bible or the Christian faith. The philosophical touchstone of Nazism was Charles Darwin's theory of evolution by natural selection. The full title of Darwin's 1859 book is *On the Origin of Species by Means of Natural Selection, or The Preservation of Favored Races in the Struggle for Life*. Hitler's own book, *Mein Kampf* (*My Struggle*), and his racist extermination policies were founded on Darwinism.

So, suggestions that Hitler was a Christian are simply wrong. But what about that claim that Nazism arose in a Christian country? Hitler's National Socialist German Workers' Party achieved power with very little help from German Christians. Hitler was never elected and never won more than 37.3 percent of the German vote. After President Hindenburg named Hitler chancellor of Germany, Hitler was able to abolish democratic institutions and become Germany's absolute dictator.[8]

The only serious opposition to Hitler in Germany came from the Evangelical Church of Germany (EKD), a federation of Lutheran and Reformed churches led by Karl Barth and Martin Niemöller. In May 1934, the EKD issued the Barmen Declaration of Faith, which rejected government control over the church. Out of the Barmen Declaration came the Confessing Church, which opposed the Nazi regime. In May 1936, the Confessing Church issued a memorandum to Hitler, denouncing his anti-Jewish and anti-Christian policies.

The Nazis arrested hundreds of Confessing Church pastors, murdered the Confessing Church's legal advisor, confiscated Confessing Church funds, and outlawed the collection of offerings in member churches. Many Confessing Church leaders ended up in prison camps, including Dietrich Bonhoeffer (who was hanged) and Martin Niemöller (who survived).

Though there were certainly wrongheaded German Christians who supported the Nazis, it is libelous to blame the church for the Holocaust. It would make as much sense as blaming American Christians for *Roe v. Wade*.

More Lessons from History

The rest of Brian McLaren's analysis of Christian history is equally flawed. He cites the Crusades as part of "the dark side of the Christian religion's track record."[9] I don't defend the atrocities committed by many of the Crusaders. In fact, in 2019 I detailed those very atrocities in my book *The Third Jihad*. But what is almost always left out of the discussion is the fact that the Crusades were a delayed response to more than four centuries of Islamic invasion, slaughter, conquest, and forced conversions. The original intent of the Crusaders was to protect defenseless Christians from being massacred or forced to convert at the point of a sword.

As historian Robert Louis Wilken writes, "By the middle of the eighth century more than fifty percent of the Christian world had fallen under Muslim rule. . . . The successors of Muhammad planted a permanent political and religious rival to Christianity and made Christians a minority in lands that had been Christian for centuries."[10] Critics of Christianity seem to forget that all the great cities that cradled the early church—Jerusalem, Damascus, Antioch, Carthage, Hippo, and Alexandria—were at one time conquered by mass slaughter and turned into strongholds of militant Islam.

Whenever the Crusades are spoken of, the full story should be told, including the story of the Islamic invasion of lands that had been peacefully converted by evangelists spreading the Good News of Jesus Christ. If you leave the Islamic conquest out of the discussion, you are not telling the truth about history.

And what about witch burnings, slavery, apartheid, and the rest of Christianity's so-called track record? Let's be honest. People have committed horrible acts in the name of the Christian religion. But the closer we adhere to God's Word and obey its teachings, the more ethical, compassionate, tolerant, and generous we will be.

Is witch burning encouraged in the Bible? Absolutely not! Is racism ever justified in Scripture? No, never. Some racists in the American South superimposed their prejudices onto the Old Testament and invented a rationalization for racism. But those rationalizations came purely from the hateful minds of those racists. They are nowhere to be found in Scripture.

The Bible and Slavery

Is slavery justified in Scripture? Many critics of Christianity point to how some Bible passages were used to condone slavery in the American South. This is an area where we need to honestly consider what the Bible does and does not say. Those who claim the Bible endorses slavery base their opinion on a casual reading of a few passages of Scripture. For example, in Ephesians, Paul writes:

> Slaves, obey your earthly masters with respect and fear, and with sincerity of heart, just as you would obey Christ. Obey them not only to win their favor when their eye is on you, but as slaves of Christ, doing the will of God from your heart. Serve wholeheartedly, as if you were serving the Lord, not people, because you know that the Lord will reward each one for whatever good they do, whether they are slave or free.[11]

Paul and Peter write similar exhortations in Colossians 3:22, 1 Timothy 6:1-2, 1 Peter 2:18, and the book of Philemon. Both accept the fact that slavery existed in that society, that it was a cultural norm during that period of history. But nowhere does Scripture say, "Slavery is ordained by God" or "Slavery is a righteous institution in society." The purpose of Paul's writing was not to critique the culture but to exhort Christians, in the real circumstances of their lives, to serve respectfully and obediently, rendering the same service they would give to the Lord himself. Paul also said:

> Masters, treat your slaves in the same way. Do not threaten them, since you know that he who is both

their Master and yours is in heaven, and there is no favoritism with him.[12]

This was a radical statement. In telling Christian masters that they should treat their slaves in a Christlike way, with kindness and compassion, Paul establishes the principle that the master-slave relationship is not one of owner to property, but of two fellow human beings made in God's image. Paul reminds the Christian masters that both they and their slaves serve the same Master in heaven. Both are equally accountable to the Lord for the conduct of their lives. This was a revolutionary concept in the first-century world.

The practice of slavery in ancient Rome and Greece was different in many ways from the practice of slavery in the American South. Greek and Roman "public slaves" worked as merchants and craftspeople in the marketplace. They earned wages, paid a regular sum to their masters, and could save money to buy their freedom. Some slaves in the ancient world were allowed to own property, hold managerial jobs, and marry and raise a family. Still, even the most privileged slaves were humiliated, stripped of dignity and liberty, treated as property, forced to work hard to enrich the owners, and were often cut off from family and country.[13]

Paul made no attempt to overturn the deeply entrenched practice of slaveholding in the first century. To do so would have been futile. It took a civil war to end slavery in nineteenth-century America, and any attempt by the early (and already persecuted) first-century church to end slavery in the Roman world would have accomplished nothing. Paul helped to change the world by spreading the gospel, not by protesting slavery. Biblical Christianity eventually helped to abolish the practice of slavery in Western society, but it did so gradually by spreading the ethical teachings of Jesus Christ.

You might ask, "Wasn't slavery practiced in ancient Israel?" Yes, but it was for different reasons and under different circumstances than slavery in the American South. Though some slaves in ancient Israel were prisoners of war, it was more common for Jewish slaves to be indentured servants of a fellow Israelite—that is, they agreed to become slaves in order to work off a debt they couldn't otherwise repay. The Old Testament law required that slaves be emancipated every seventh year.[14]

The Golden Rule that Jesus established—"Do to others as you would have them do to you"[15]—is one Christian concept that helped to undermine the institution of slavery. Paul's teachings about human equality also chipped away at the arguments for slavery: "There is neither Jew nor Gentile, neither slave nor free, nor is there male and female, for you are all one in Christ Jesus."[16] Over time, people who had grown up accepting slavery as normal began to see it as morally abhorrent.

Closer to our day, the Second Great Awakening—an evangelical revival movement in America in the early nineteenth century—stirred a wave of abolitionism across America. The great soul-winning revivalist Charles Finney was also one of America's great abolitionists and social reformers. The abolitionist preacher Theodore Weld wrote an influential book called *The Bible against Slavery*, in which he laid out the biblical case against slavery from the Old Testament. One Bible passage that influenced and motivated the abolitionists was this statement from the apostle Paul:

> We also know that the law is made not for the righteous but for lawbreakers and rebels, the ungodly and sinful, the unholy and irreligious, for those who kill their fathers or mothers, for murderers, for the sexually immoral, for those practicing homosexuality, for slave traders and liars and perjurers—and for whatever else is contrary to the sound doctrine.[17]

In that list of sins and crimes is the term *slave traders*. Other translations use a different term, such as *enslavers* or *kidnappers* or *menstealers*. The term refers to the practice of kidnapping people and selling them into slavery, which was the foundation of the slave trade in early America. If not for the practice of kidnapping black Africans, the slave plantations of the South could not have existed. Paul, writing to his protégé Timothy, laid the moral foundation for the abolition of slave trading and slaveholding. For Paul, trafficking in human misery was on the same level as murder and sexual immorality. Slave owners who tried to justify their crimes from the Bible could find no loophole in that verse.

The Bible accepts as reality many practices that God hates, including slavery, polygamy, and divorce. God hates divorce because of the harm it inflicts on those who are divorced and their children.[18] Yet the Bible also makes provision for divorce in certain circumstances. Why? Because God's Word realistically deals with situations God does not approve of and does not endorse. As Jesus explained, "Moses permitted you to divorce your wives because your hearts were hard. But it was not this way from the beginning."[19]

In the same way, the Bible accepts the reality of slavery but never approves of it. God always endorses freedom: "Now the Lord is the Spirit, and where the Spirit of the Lord is, there is freedom."[20] Slavery is a crime against God and humanity. The entire European-American slave-based economy was unbiblical and immoral. The Bible-believing abolitionists knew without a doubt that slavery must be abolished, and in reliance upon God they achieved that goal.

Abandoning the World's Only Hope

By now it should be clear why we *must* hold to the teachings of the Bible. Wrestle with them if you must, but don't abandon them or disobey them. The moment we think we can pick and choose which Scripture passages to obey and which to ignore, which ones are valid and which ones are not, we find ourselves sinking in moral and spiritual quicksand. Either be a Christian and submit to the authority of *all* of God's Word—or reject it and admit you're in rebellion against God's authority.

Don't try to have it both ways. Don't use selected bits and pieces of the Bible to endorse your worldly social and political agenda while denying the inspiration and authority of the entire text. Jesus is assembling a Kingdom made up of "a great multitude that no one [can] count, from every nation, tribe, people and language,"[21] dwelling together in peace, harmony, and joy. His Kingdom is not of this world. It is not beholden to any political party or social ideology. His Kingdom is not a democracy in which we get to vote for the parts of the Bible we approve of.

Jesus is the King of kings, the Lord of lords. His Kingdom is a theocratic monarchy, and in his Kingdom, his word is final, his authority absolute.

The Bible is God's self-revelation. It reveals his mind, his will, and his character. God is the ultimate judge of the form and content of his Word—not us. Jesus is truth incarnate, the Logos, the Word, the perfect expression of God's self-revealing truth.

The progressive "Christians" complain that the Bible is not inclusive enough. Brian McLaren writes that biblical, evangelical Christianity has "shown a pervasive disdain for other religions of the world," whose members we should view "not as enemies but as beloved neighbors, and whenever possible, as dialogue partners and even collaborators."[22]

In a post-Christian, post-truth world, partnering with other belief systems may sound tolerant and open-minded. But the Christian faith does not contain *partial* truth that must be augmented by truth from other religions. Yes, Jesus calls us to love people of other religions and people of no religion at all. He has commissioned us to preach the Good News of Jesus Christ to everyone. But we must never become partners or collaborators with error and falsehood. We must never deny, diminish, or dilute the bold, unambiguous claim of Jesus: "I am the way and the truth and the life. No one comes to the Father except through me."[23]

The inclusiveness the progressive "Christians" promote is modern-day idolatry. It is the sin of spiritual adultery that the apostle James warns about: "You adulterous people, don't you know that friendship with the world means enmity against God? Therefore, anyone who chooses to be a friend of the world becomes an enemy of God."[24]

No wonder so many progressive "Christians" today reject any expression of doctrinal certainty. No wonder they mischaracterize faithful humility before the authority of God's Word as arrogance. No wonder they use euphemistic phrases such as "the Easter story" instead of boldly, confidently proclaiming the resurrection of Jesus as truth. No wonder they recoil from the very thought of *absolutes* and *objective truth*. No wonder some of them embrace moral relativism and a completely secular view of sexual ethics.

That's why Jude exhorts us to *contend* for the faith that was once for all entrusted to us. The false teaching and apostasy we see in our time is nothing new. From the earliest days of the church, Satan has waged an all-out assault on God's truth. In fact, most of the New Testament epistles were written to combat various forces of deception that had infiltrated the church.

Satan understands that the most effective way to destroy the church is from the inside out, not the outside in. That's why these postmodern, post-evangelical, progressive Trojan horses keep slipping through our gates to catch us unaware.

That's why Peter tells us, "Be alert and of sober mind. Your enemy the devil prowls around like a roaring lion looking for someone to devour. Resist him, standing firm in the faith."[25]

What makes the abandonment of God's truth so tragic and senseless is that the Bible contains the solutions to all the problems the progressive "Christians" claim to want to solve. If you want to reform society, if you want to help the poor and liberate the oppressed, if you want to heal the planet, start with the gospel of Jesus Christ. Secular-left social programs and human-designed social gospel are all doomed to fail. For two thousand years, the gospel has proved to be the only agenda that transforms lives and society. It is unbelievably foolish to abandon the world's only true hope, the gospel of Jesus Christ. Yet that is precisely what the progressive "Christians" are determined to do.

The gospel transforms society on a large scale by changing one life at a time. When Christians live out the great commission given to us by Jesus, the gospel spreads at an exponential rate, transforming a godless society into a community of Jesus-followers. Instead of trying to force the levers of worldly power to achieve change, we can change lives from the inside through the power of the Holy Spirit.

Let me show you how exponential growth works.

Suppose I made you an offer: You can either have one million dollars in cash, payable in thirty days, or you can have a penny today, two pennies tomorrow, four pennies the next day, eight pennies the next, doubling each day for thirty days. Which offer would you take?

If, like me, you're not very good at math, you might be

tempted to take the million dollars. But what if you took the pennies instead? By day seven, you would have a measly 64 cents. By day fourteen, you'd have $81.92. By day twenty-one, you'd still have only $10,485.76. But on day twenty-eight—look out! You'd have $1,342,177.28! And on day thirty? $5,368,709.12. You'd be more than five times better off taking the pennies instead of the million dollars.

Now suppose that, instead of pennies, we are talking about people. You start with one Christian, and he or she shares the gospel with a friend, and that person follows Christ. Now you have two Christians. The next day, they each win a soul to the Lord—four Christians. Those four Christians each win a soul to the Lord, and now you have eight. And so on and so on. That's exponential growth, and that's how the early church spread so quickly in the first century. Whenever God brings revival to a church or a community, you always see that kind of rapid, exponential growth. That's Kingdom mathematics.

I know that some people get an endorphin rush from marching and protesting and trying to persuade governments and institutions to accede to their demands. But if you want to experience a *real* spiritual high, tell people about Jesus. And if you truly want to change the world, proclaim the Good News every day to everyone you meet.

A King, Not a Social Reformer

Progressive "Christians" claim that the gospel is *not* the Good News of eternal life through faith in Christ. They claim that the gospel is the message that "the kingdom of heaven is at hand."[26] By this they mean that we are to build the Kingdom of Heaven in the here and now (which is how they interpret the phrase "at hand"). We do this, they say, by adopting programs and practices and behaviors that are essentially social and political in nature.

The progressives tell us that we must work individually and collectively to promote "justice" (which they define as a more equal distribution of wealth and opportunities, along with building coalitions among social groups such as ethnic minorities or gay people). They also say we must join together to pressure the government and other institutions into supporting the progressive agenda. Progressive "Christians" don't believe that the gospel is capable of changing society. That's why they seek political leverage to achieve their goals. That's what Brian McLaren means when he belittles the gospel as "information on how to go to heaven after you die" with a tiny footnote on "social/global transformation."[27]

To the progressive "Christians," personal salvation has no value. The progressives' "kingdom of heaven" is an earthly political and institutional kingdom. The kingdom is "at hand"—it can be built in the here and now—by applying a spiritual veneer to the secular-left agenda.

For example, Brian McLaren writes that, before his conversion from evangelical Christianity to progressive "Christianity," he believed in personal salvation: "I often spoke of Jesus as my 'personal Savior,' and I urged others to believe in Jesus in the same way."[28]

After converting to progressive "Christianity," McLaren

redefined *salvation* in a way that excludes eternal life in heaven with Jesus: "I still believe that Jesus is vitally interested in saving me and you by individually judging us, by forgiving us of our wrongs, and teaching us to live in a better way."[29] Salvation, as redefined by Brian McLaren, means being judged and forgiven for not living out the progressive social and political agenda in the past, and it means living "a better way," the progressive way, in the present and future.

But Jesus said, "My kingdom is not of this world."[30] He did not come as a social reformer or a political activist. He came as the King of kings and Lord of lords. His gospel of salvation not only changes lives; it transforms societies and nations. Century after century, the pure truth of the Christian gospel has produced the very social transformation the progressives say they want.

It was biblical Christianity, not progressive "Christianity," that inspired John Wesley, John Newton, William Wilberforce, Harriet Beecher Stowe, and Charles Haddon Spurgeon to battle the scourge of human slavery. It was biblical Christianity, not progressive "Christianity," that led the Christian abolitionist Jonathan Blanchard to found Wheaton College in 1860 as a nondenominational Christian institution of higher learning. (Wheaton also served as a stop on the anti-slavery Underground Railroad.)

It was biblical Christianity, not progressive "Christianity," that established the first hospitals and universities in the world. It was biblical Christianity, not progressive "Christianity," that emboldened Dr. Martin Luther King Jr. to put his life on the line for the cause of civil rights. It was biblical

Christianity, not progressive "Christianity," that founded a network of crisis pregnancy centers to offer women and girls a caring Christian alternative to the callous exploitation of their bodies by the abortion industry.

Let's look at two of the social issues on the progressive "Christian" agenda and ask ourselves which gospel is better equipped to solve these problems—the biblical gospel of salvation by grace through faith in Jesus Christ or the social gospel of the progressive "Christians."

Saving the Environment?

Writing as a former evangelical, Rachel Held Evans said, "We sneered at the notion of climate change yet believed that God once made the earth stand still."[31] And Jim Wallis of *Sojourners* magazine wrote in the *Huffington Post*, "Stand up for the reality of climate change. If we say we love God and care for God's creation, it is time to raise our voices over the crisis of climate change."[32]

Though evangelical Christians are often caricatured as having no respect for the environment, the Christians I know are diligent about recycling, conserving resources, avoiding waste, and respecting the planet we all share. Brian McLaren calls the evangelical view a "skyhook Second Coming, wrapping up the whole of creation like an empty candy wrapper and throwing it in the cosmic dumpster so God can finally bring our souls to heaven."[33] I have never heard an evangelical Christian express such an attitude. As biblical Christians, we know that the Lord may return today or a thousand years from now. In the meantime, God calls us to live faithfully, take care of his creation, and proclaim the Good News of Jesus Christ. The Bible teaches us to respect the world God created: "The LORD God took the man and put him in the Garden of Eden to work it *and take care of it.*"[34] The Bible also teaches us virtues of self-discipline, courtesy, responsibility for oneself, and consideration for others. Trashing the environment is disrespectful to God, to his creation, and to the people who would have to clean it up.

Are many Christians suspicious of the progressive environmental agenda? Absolutely. We don't know if the United Nations' Intergovernmental Panel on Climate Change and similar groups are telling us the truth about global warming. We are troubled that their scientific claims always come wrapped in a socialist ideology.

For example, the United Nations' "Sustainable Development Goals Knowledge Platform" sets forth a Marxist agenda of wealth redistribution: "Sustained, inclusive, and sustainable economic growth is essential for prosperity. This will only be possible if wealth is shared and income inequality is addressed. . . . We commit to making fundamental changes in the way that our societies produce and consume goods and services."[35]

In 1996, five years after the collapse of the Soviet Union, former Soviet president Mikhail Gorbachev spoke of using the "crisis" of global warming to scare the nations of the world into accepting strong international controls. He said, "The threat of environmental crisis will be the international disaster key to unlock the New World Order."[36]

Timothy Wirth, former undersecretary of state for global issues in the Clinton administration, told a Climate Summit audience, "We have got to ride the global warming issue. Even if the theory of global warming is wrong, we will be doing the right thing in terms of economic policy and environmental policy."[37] Many Christians love the environment God made but are skeptical of the secular left's Marxist, socialist, anti-Western ideology that comes packaged with the green agenda.

Saving the Poor?

Both Bible-believing evangelical Christians and post-evangelical progressive "Christians" believe that God is on the side of the poor. Both believe it is a biblical imperative that we help meet the needs of the poor. Both sides agree on the goal—to eliminate poverty—but disagree on the means to achieve that goal. Evangelicals believe Jesus has called the church to help the poor. Progressives want the government to do the church's job.

Jesus, in his Olivet discourse, spoke of his future return to judge the world, when he will say to the righteous, "Take your inheritance, the kingdom prepared for you since the creation of the world. For I was hungry and you gave me something to eat, I was thirsty and you gave me something to drink, I was a stranger and you invited me in, I needed clothes and you clothed me, I was sick and you looked after me, I was in prison and you came to visit me. . . . Truly I tell you, whatever you did for one of the least of these brothers and sisters of mine, you did for me."[38]

Our Lord calls us to reach out to the poor with compassion, generosity, and the Good News of Jesus Christ. Once, when Jesus attended a banquet at the home of a prominent Pharisee, he said to his host, "When you give a luncheon or dinner, do not invite your friends, your brothers or sisters, your relatives, or your rich neighbors; if you do, they may invite you back and so you will be repaid. But when you give a banquet, invite the poor, the crippled, the lame, the blind, and you will be blessed. Although they cannot repay you, you will be repaid at the resurrection of the righteous."[39]

In his parable of the Good Samaritan, Jesus vividly illustrated his view of our ethical responsibility to the less fortunate and the despised among us, and then he told us to "go and do likewise."[40]

Jesus says we are to get personally involved in the needs and sufferings of this world. We are to live generously and compassionately. We are to give of our own time, our own resources, our own love and tears, to meet the needs of the poor and the oppressed.

Now, I'm sure that progressive "Christians" give of their time and possessions to help the poor. I'm not accusing anyone of hypocrisy here. They have good intentions. But when they abandon the gospel of salvation and instead preach a gospel of social and political activism, they have corrupted the gospel. They have replaced the Good News of Jesus Christ with a well-intentioned but worldly agenda.

Progressives can sometimes be found marching, protesting, demanding a change in government policies. A favorite slogan of theirs is "a budget is a moral document." Why do progressive "Christians" invest so much time and effort in pressuring the government and promoting higher federal spending? I believe it's because they have lost faith in the gospel that transforms human hearts. They have lost confidence in the Kingdom that is not of this world. So they march and protest and demand that the worldly kingdom—the government—do the work that Jesus entrusted to his church, the ministry of feeding the hungry, giving drink to the thirsty, and clothing the unclothed.

And this is important to understand: When we talk about the government, we are talking about the taxpayers. When progressive "Christians" take to the streets of Washington, DC, to demand more federal spending for social programs, they are saying, in effect, "We want the taxpayers to feed the poor and clothe the naked. We want the taxpayers to do the job Jesus assigned to the church."

The government can issue a welfare check, but can the government dispense caring and compassion to the poor? Can the government listen to a poor person's problems and fears? Can the government share the Good News of Jesus Christ? Progressive "Christians" feel that if they've pushed the levers of worldly power and enlarged the federal welfare budget, they've really accomplished something for the Kingdom of God.

Don't get me wrong. I'm happy when truly needy people get a portion of the taxes I pay. I strongly suspect that the government does a poor job of determining who the truly needy are, but that's a different discussion. In obedience to God's Word, I faithfully render unto Caesar the things that are Caesar's, and I pray that the government will use my taxes for the common good. America is a compassionate country because it was founded on Christian principles. But God never intended for the secular government to take over the ministry of the church.

For the sake of argument, let's say the federal budget is a "moral document," as the progressive "Christians" claim. Very well. If the government decides to spend more on social programs, is the budget automatically more *moral*? Increased spending requires higher taxes, which means a greater burden on the middle class, slower job creation, and higher unemployment. Is that *moral*? If we don't raise taxes, then the government must borrow more money. In February 2019, the national debt passed the $22 trillion mark.[41] Do progressives want the government to spend money it doesn't have when our nation is already perilously deep in debt? Is that *moral*?

Who is going to pay back the $22 trillion (and counting) that the government has borrowed? Answer: our children, grandchildren, and great grandchildren. We are spending money we don't have, and we are sticking future generations with the bill. Is that *moral*? Admiral Michael Mullen, former chairman of the Joint Chiefs of Staff, has called the national debt the greatest threat to our national security. And when former defense secretary James Mattis testified before a congressional committee, he said, "I consider it [an] abrogation of our generation's responsibility to transfer a debt of this size to our children."[42] Is an out-of-control national debt *moral*?

I don't agree that it is moral to demand that the government do the work of the church. We are individually and collectively responsible as Christians to obey the will of our Lord Jesus Christ. He said, "If anyone gives even a cup of cold water to one of these little ones who is my disciple, truly I tell you, that person will certainly not lose their reward."[43]

When Jesus spoke with the Samaritan woman at the well, he told her that he offered her "living water." Everyone who drinks water from a well in the ground, he said, will be thirsty again, "but whoever drinks the water I give them will never thirst. Indeed, the water I give them will become in them a spring of water welling up to eternal life."[44]

In God's economy, there's a big difference between a cup of cold water dispensed in the name of the government and a cup of cold water offered in Jesus' name. When a Christian gives a cup of cold water to a thirsty person, that cup is always accompanied by something vastly more important, eternal, and satisfying than mere H_2O. It is accompanied by *living water*.

The Bible is the only truly moral document I trust. It is living water for thirsty souls. It is good news for hungry hearts. It is an agenda of social and global transformation through the preaching of the gospel. It impacts history and changes society—one human soul at a time.

PART TWO

A CHRISTIANITY WITHOUT COMPROMISE

I Believe in God the Father

In 1987, we founded The Church of The Apostles in Atlanta with fewer than forty adult members. We never dreamed we would grow to become a congregation of more than three thousand souls.

We did not choose the name of our church. That name was given to us by the man who had authority over me in the denomination we belonged to at that time. He named our church The Church of The Apostles as an act of mockery and derision. In that mainline Protestant denomination, our church was one of a dwindling number of congregations that still held to the foundational teaching of the apostles.

Sadly, like most leaders in that denomination, the man in authority over me did not believe that the Bible is the inspired Word of God. He did not believe that Jesus is the crucified and resurrected Son of God, and the only way to God the Father. He did not believe in salvation by grace through faith in Jesus Christ.

He told me, "We don't need evangelicals and gospel-preaching churches in our denomination. The only reason we are permitting you to start this church is that we know it will fail. Here are two things I want you to remember: First, don't quit your day job. This church will close its doors in less than six months. Second, since you and your church members are so big on believing the Bible and spreading the gospel, we will name your congregation The Church of The Apostles."

"I am under authority," I said. "I accept your direction, and we will call ourselves The Church of The Apostles."

The name that man gave to our church, which he intended as mockery, has proven to be a name of blessing. He intended it for evil, but God has used it for good.

In a post-Christian, post-truth culture that chases after false gospels and delusional beliefs, we continue to teach, preach, and bear witness to the biblical and historical meaning of the gospel of Jesus Christ. A biblical faith takes the Bible at its word and doesn't add anything or subtract anything. We continue "to contend for the faith that was once for all entrusted to God's holy people."[1]

Where do the advocates for the many new forms of "Christianity" go wrong? They tend to veer off in one direction or another from the essential, orthodox, biblical understanding of what it means to believe in Jesus Christ. They are so intently focused on so-called *social justice* that they never bother to tell the poor and oppressed how to be justified by faith. They spend so much time railing against economic poverty that they haven't a word to say about spiritual poverty.

One of the purest summations of the Christian faith is found in the Apostles' Creed, written nearly two thousand years ago. Originally composed in either Latin or Greek, it is the oldest statement of faith in the Christian world, and it encompasses all the essential doctrines laid down in the four Gospels, the New Testament letters, and parts of the Old Testament. If we hold fast to the Apostles' Creed, we will remain grounded in God's truth, and we will never be confused by false teachers and pseudo-Christianity. As Albert Mohler writes in *The Apostles' Creed: Discovering Authentic Christianity in an Age of Counterfeits*:

> From its earliest beginnings the church has faced the dual challenge of affirming the truth and confronting error. Over the centuries, the church has turned to a series of creeds and confessions of faith in order to define and defend true Christianity. The confession of faith we know as the Apostles' Creed is one of the most important of these confessions. For long, unbroken centuries it has stood as one of the most crucial teaching instruments of the Christian faith—along with the Ten Commandments and the Lord's Prayer.[2]

It's true, the church has been assailed by false doctrine ever since its founding. The apostasy of the progressive "Christians" is nothing new. Spiritual defection is older than Christianity itself, as old as the first lie whispered in Eden. So it's important to remind ourselves of the rock-solid doctrinal pillars of our faith.

There are many peripheral beliefs over which Christians may reasonably disagree, such as the structure of a church government or the precise mode of baptism. But the Apostles' Creed is the ground floor of Christian belief. You cannot deny any of its statements without toppling the entire structure. There is unity and fellowship among all Christians who sincerely affirm the Apostles' Creed.

"I Believe in God, the Father Almighty"

Just as the Christian faith has been Trinitarian since its inception, the Apostles' Creed is structured in a triune form, affirming faith in (1) God the Father, (2) Jesus Christ the Son, and (3) the Holy Spirit. According to tradition, each of the twelve apostles contributed one doctrinal principle, and all twelve doctrines make up the creed.

I believe in God, the Father almighty,
Creator of heaven and earth.

I believe in Jesus Christ, his only Son, our Lord,
who was conceived by the Holy Spirit
and born of the virgin Mary.

He suffered under Pontius Pilate,
was crucified, died, and was buried;
he descended to hell.
The third day he rose again from the dead.
He ascended to heaven
and is seated at the right hand of God the Father
almighty.
From there he will come to judge the living and
the dead.

I believe in the Holy Spirit,
the holy catholic church,
the communion of saints,
the forgiveness of sins,
the resurrection of the body,
and the life everlasting. Amen.

The Apostles' Creed begins with a simple declarative statement: "I believe in God." This is the foundation of everything else we believe. The entire doctrinal structure of the Christian faith is built on those four words.

The next phrase begins to unfold the true nature of God, "the Father almighty." God is our Father. He has generated us and made us in his image. He provides for us and cares for us, instructs us and blesses us. He wants the best for us, and he seeks to bring us to a place of maturity. He is our role model, the one we seek to imitate and emulate.

When Jesus taught us to pray, "Our Father who art in heaven," he wasn't teaching us to think of God as an abstract symbol. He was teaching us to relate to God in the most real and personal sense possible—as our Father. His love, care, and provision for us are far beyond anything we can imagine.

Calling God "the Father" does not mean he is *male* as human beings understand gender. "God is spirit," Jesus says in John 4:24. Both men and women are made in the image of God. When the Bible refers to God by the pronouns *he* or *him*, it speaks of God's personhood, not his gender. God himself once said to Israel, "As a mother comforts her child, so will I comfort you."[3] All the best qualities of both male and female are found in God. He is the living definition of the perfect parent, and a role model for godly fathers and mothers.

The Apostles' Creed calls God *almighty*. His might, wisdom, and power created the universe and created you and me. Though he is our Father, we must never forget that he is "Father almighty." We must never take him for granted. His name is holy, and his majesty is beyond our comprehension. Thus, it is all the more amazing to know that this awesome God is our Father almighty, that we are his beloved, and as his children we now have free access to the throne room of the King of kings. We can address the King of the universe as "our Father." There is no greater privilege than that.

"Creator of Heaven and Earth"

The Bible opens with the story of "God, the Father almighty, Creator of heaven and earth." With his word, Genesis tells us, he called the universe into existence from nothing. He hung the stars and planets like Christmas tree ornaments upon the emptiness of space. He reshaped the formless earth into a masterpiece of dazzling color and beauty. He divided the land from the waters and the earth from the sky. Then the Father almighty brought forth life in all its myriad forms upon the earth—creatures that swim, crawl, slither, walk, and fly. As the centerpiece of his beautiful creation, he made a lush and fertile garden, which he called Eden. In that garden, God placed the first man, Adam. And from Adam's side, he fashioned the first woman, Eve.

Why did God create Adam and Eve? He made them so that he could share his love, goodness, and everlasting joy with them. All of God's creation, including the first man and the first woman in their unfallen state, manifested God's glory and wisdom. As the psalmist David writes, "I praise you because I am fearfully and wonderfully made; your works are wonderful, I know that full well."[4]

Adam and Eve enjoyed daily fellowship with their Father-Creator. They enjoyed all the delights of the Garden of Eden but one: God said, "You must not eat from the tree of the knowledge of good and evil, for when you eat from it you will certainly die."[5] Adam and Eve had the gift of free will. They had absolute freedom to obey or disobey God.

They lived a wonderfully pleasant life in their earthly paradise—until the beginning of Genesis 3, when Satan the tempter, in the form of a serpent, entered the garden. The plan Satan employed in the garden is the same plan he still uses against you and me today. He didn't slander God or attack God. He simply asked questions and made suggestions: "Did God really say, 'You must not eat from any tree in the garden'? . . . You will not certainly die. . . . For God knows that when you eat from it your eyes will be opened, and you will be like God, knowing good and evil."[6]

Today that same voice says, "Surely Jesus can't be the only way to God, can he? If you are a sincere Buddhist or Muslim, God surely wouldn't cast you out, would he? God isn't narrow-minded or intolerant, is he?" These glib, wise-sounding lies come from the same tempter who seduced Eve.

When Adam and Eve tasted the fruit, they realized that there are tragic consequences for disobeying God's commands. There are tragic consequences to believing the lie and defecting from the truth. The moment they violated God's word and tasted the fruit, their close fellowship with God was broken. Suddenly, they became afraid of God—and they were ashamed. They tried to cover their nakedness, and they attempted to hide from his sight. Thousands of years later, you and I still live in the shadow of their tragic choice.

God, the Father almighty, Creator of heaven and earth, gave us the Genesis account so that we would know who made us, why there is sin in the world, why we are helpless to save ourselves, and why we need a Savior. In the book of Genesis, we learn that we are sons of Adam and daughters of Eve. We learn that the yearnings we so often feel but cannot name are truly yearnings to return to the garden—yearnings for our home in heaven.

Today we live in a hostile world, the world that Adam and Eve made by their willful, sinful choice. After Adam and Eve were exiled, they and all their descendants were condemned to a life of miserable labor to coax a little food from the thorn-infested ground. The children of Adam and Eve multiplied the sins and sorrows of their parents. Adam and Eve grew old, and just as God had warned, they died.

The human race grew in numbers and increased in sin and rebellion against God. They built a civilization that was openly defiant toward God. That is the civilization we live in today.

Though many claim the account of Adam and Eve is nothing more than a quaint fable, the biblical account of the creation and fall of humanity holds the key to the human condition. It explains our human brilliance and creativity—we were created in the image of God. It explains our human depravity, cruelty, folly, and hate—God's image in us has been marred by sin. We know we were created for the garden, yet Adam's sin turned us out into the wilderness.

Though the Genesis story is ancient beyond human memory, it is still relevant to our lives in the twenty-first century. Not only does it tell the story of the greatest tragedy in human history, but it also contains the seeds of our hope of redemption. In Genesis 3:15, God says to the serpent:

> I will put enmity
>> between you and the woman,
>> and between your offspring and hers;
> he will crush your head,
>> and you will strike his heel.

Here in the opening pages of the Bible, we see the first prophetic promise of a coming Savior. Who is the offspring of the woman? It is Jesus. In vivid symbols, God foretells the Crucifixion—and it is fascinating to note that God speaks this prophecy not to Adam and Eve, but to Satan! God is pronouncing Satan's doom. Centuries later, when Jesus is nailed to a Roman cross outside of Jerusalem, the serpent will strike his heel. He will inflict pain, torture, spiritual agony, and death on Jesus. But the moment Jesus gives up his spirit and takes his final breath, he will crush the head of Satan.

All this truth is contained in that one verse in Genesis 3. Later, God will speak through Old Testament prophets and reveal additional glimpses of the coming Messiah. And in the fullness of time, the offspring of the woman will be born in Bethlehem. He will grow and preach and work wonders and die and rise again, and God's prophecy to the serpent in Genesis 3:15 will be fulfilled.

To anyone who thinks the account of Adam and Eve is a myth, I would point out that if you remove that story from the book of Genesis, you will not be able to make sense of the rest of the Bible. You will not even be able to make sense of your own life. You will certainly not be able to make sense of the gospel and God's plan for human history and his plan of salvation.

From Genesis to Revelation, God's inspired Word is a unified whole, a systematic explanation of the human tragedy and of God's plan of redemption. The Word of God stands like a strong, towering, well-constructed fortress. And the entire structure rests upon the foundation of the Creation story.

We believe in God, the Father almighty, Creator of heaven and earth. He has told us his story, and it is not a myth. He has written this story on the pages of time and space and human history. He has revealed himself to us as the almighty Creator and as a loving and forgiving Father. The better we get to know God, the Father almighty, the better we are able to understand ourselves.

Between the Bookends

The story of Genesis and the story of Revelation are the bookends of human history. All the achievements and atrocities of humanity, all human aspiration and human degradation, all human triumph and human tragedy, take place between the first chapter of Genesis and the final chapter of Revelation.

Those two books are mirror images of each other. The story of humanity's creation begins with a beautiful garden and a tree of life. The story begins with human beings living in perfect fellowship with God, the Father almighty, Creator of heaven and earth.

The end of human history, as foretold in the book of Revelation, is the story of the resurrected saints of God living joyfully in the New Jerusalem, a beautiful garden city with a tree of life—a city that descends from heaven:

> Then the angel showed me the river of the water of life, as clear as crystal, flowing from the throne of God and of the Lamb down the middle of the great street of the city. On each side of the river stood the

tree of life, bearing twelve crops of fruit, yielding its fruit every month. And the leaves of the tree are for the healing of the nations. No longer will there be any curse.[7]

When the throne of God is established in the eternal city, the curse of sin will be lifted forever. The innocence and fellowship that was lost in the Garden of Eden will be restored at the end of time in the garden of the New Jerusalem.

The book of Genesis contains the account of the first wedding—the marriage of Adam and Eve. It's a simple ceremony, conducted without organ music, a minister, or even a wedding dress. But it is performed in the sight of the only witness who matters—God, the Father almighty, Creator of heaven and earth. Genesis records the simple wedding vows:

The man said,

> "This is now bone of my bones
> and flesh of my flesh;
> she shall be called 'woman,'
> for she was taken out of man."

That is why a man leaves his father and mother and is united to his wife, and they become one flesh.[8]

In the book of Revelation, we find a striking parallel to the wedding account in Genesis. It is the marriage of the Bridegroom, the Lord Jesus, and his bride—believers from every tribe and nation, from every era of history, who by faith placed their trust in God to provide the perfect sacrifice for sin. John, the writer of the book of Revelation, describes the wedding:

> "Let us rejoice and be glad
>   and give him glory!
> For the wedding of the Lamb has come,
>   and his bride has made herself ready.
> Fine linen, bright and clean,
>   was given her to wear."

(Fine linen stands for the righteous acts of God's holy people.)

Then the angel said to me, "Write this: Blessed are those who are invited to the wedding supper of the Lamb!" And he added, "These are the true words of God."[9]

And there are still more parallels between Genesis and Revelation. In Genesis, God, the Father almighty, Creator of heaven and earth, gave human beings authority over his creation: "The LORD God took the man and put him in the Garden of Eden to work it and take care of it."[10] In Revelation, God the Father gives his people authority to reign over his new creation with Jesus.

The Genesis account begins with the creation of Adam and Eve in a place of peace, joy, and fellowship with God. Revelation closes with all the redeemed of humanity entering a place of heavenly peace, joy, and fellowship with God. In

Genesis, God sentences Satan to eternal death; in Revelation, God carries out that sentence.

I believe in God, the Father almighty, Creator of heaven and earth. I believe in the account of his works in Genesis and Revelation. During the time between Genesis and Revelation, something amazing happened that altered the course of history. Somehow, God solved the sin problem that began in Genesis 3. Somehow, God intervened in human history to cure our inherited spiritual disorder and heal us of sin and death.

What did God do? We find the answer in the second section of the Apostles' Creed.

I Believe in Jesus the Son

A number of years ago, an author named Betty Eadie appeared on the *Oprah Winfrey Show* to tout a book called *Embraced by the Light*. She claimed she'd had a near-death experience at age thirty-one. By her account, she saw Jesus while she was "dead," and she returned to tell the world that death is nothing to fear and that everyone goes to heaven.

Oprah said, "I believe that there are many paths to God. . . . I certainly don't believe there is only one way. . . . Did Jesus indicate that to you?"

"Absolutely," Eadie said, adding, "I was experiencing something that was absolutely different than I had been taught in *any* of the churches."

"Well," Oprah said, "I'm glad to hear that, because if Jesus is as cool as I think he is, he would have had to tell you that."[1]

I don't know if Jesus is "cool," but I do know that Jesus never contradicts himself. He would never tell a woman in a "near-death experience" the exact opposite of what he says in John 14:6: "I am the way and the truth and the life. No one comes to the Father except through me." Anyone who claims otherwise is either deceived or dishonest.

This is a serious matter. Your eternal destiny depends on whether you embrace or reject the claims of Jesus Christ. The world says there are many paths to God. The progressive "Christians" say there are many paths to God. But Jesus says there is no way to be saved apart from him. As Peter courageously told the angry, murderous leaders of the Sanhedrin, "Salvation is found in no one else, for there is no other name under heaven given to mankind by which we must be saved."[2]

You may be sincere in your beliefs. You may try to live a moral life. You may try to be kind and forgiving and generous toward everyone around you. You may be the most sincere person who ever lived. But if you are sincerely wrong about Jesus, your sincerity won't save you. That's why it's so important to know who Jesus is and why the truth about Jesus matters. We find the truth about Jesus in the middle section of the Apostles' Creed:

I believe in Jesus Christ, his only Son, our Lord,
who was conceived by the Holy Spirit
and born of the virgin Mary.

He suffered under Pontius Pilate,
was crucified, died, and was buried;
he descended to hell.
The third day he rose again from the dead.
He ascended to heaven
and is seated at the right hand of God the Father
almighty.
From there he will come to judge the living and
the dead.

That is a lot of truth to take in! For two thousand years, false teachers have tried to twist and distort and reshape Jesus to fit their personal biases or to promote some new gospel, some new kind of Christianity. I've heard people preach about "the historical Jesus" or "Jesus the revolutionary" or "the Marxist Jesus" or "Jesus the positive thinker" or "Jesus the enlightenment philosopher" or "Jesus the mystic."

But the Jesus of the Bible—the Jesus who is the way, the truth, and the life—is not hard to find. In fact, we find him perfectly described in the Apostles' Creed.

"I Believe in Jesus Christ, His Only Son, Our Lord"

We often hear that Jesus was a great moral teacher like Socrates or Aristotle—but that he was not the Son of God. We hear that *nobody* believes in miracles anymore. Skeptics and progressives like to focus on the "historical Jesus"—a non-miraculous Jesus, a Jesus who was not born of a virgin, who never turned water into wine, who never walked on water, who never healed the sick or raised the dead, and who was never resurrected.

Many people who do not believe in the Jesus of the Bible still celebrate Christmas and Easter. They enjoy the holiday sentiments of peace on earth, goodwill toward men. They quote the teachings of Jesus from the Sermon on the Mount, but they don't like to talk about his other teachings, such as "You must be born again."[3]

The Apostles' Creed requires us to embrace *all* the teachings of Jesus, including all that he taught about himself. If we hold to the teachings of Jesus, then we are truly his disciples. If we reject or compromise his teachings and his claims, then we have no right to call ourselves Christians. In John's Gospel, Jesus offers seven confirmations, or proofs, that he is the long-awaited Messiah, the Son of God.

First confirmation: God the Father

Jesus said, "The Father who sent me has himself testified concerning me."[4] Jesus is referring to a specific event that occurred immediately after he was baptized in the Jordan River by John the Baptist:

> As soon as Jesus was baptized, he went up out of the water. At that moment heaven was opened, and he saw the Spirit of God descending like a dove and alighting on him. And a voice from heaven said, "This is my Son, whom I love; with him I am well pleased."[5]

John the Baptist and a crowd of witnesses heard the voice of the Father affirming that Jesus is his Son. The Father announced that a special father/son relationship existed between himself and Jesus of Nazareth.

On another occasion, Jesus took three of his closest followers up onto a high mountain. The Gospel of Mark tells us:

> After six days Jesus took Peter, James and John with him and led them up a high mountain, where they were all alone. There he was transfigured before them. His clothes became dazzling white, whiter than anyone in the world could bleach them. And there appeared before them Elijah and Moses, who were talking with Jesus.
>
> Peter said to Jesus, "Rabbi, it is good for us to be here. Let us put up three shelters—one for you, one for Moses and one for Elijah." (He did not know what to say, they were so frightened.)
>
> Then a cloud appeared and covered them, and a voice came from the cloud: "This is my Son, whom I love. Listen to him!"
>
> Suddenly, when they looked around, they no longer saw anyone with them except Jesus.[6]

As Jesus talked with Moses and Elijah, God spoke and confirmed that Jesus was his beloved Son. Jesus did not merely *claim* to be the Son of God. The Father *proclaimed* Jesus as his Son, and the Father's proclamation was heard by many witnesses.

Second confirmation: The Holy Spirit

Matthew 3:16 tells us that Jesus, at his baptism, "saw the Spirit of God descending like a dove and alighting on him." The Spirit confirmed Jesus as the Son of God by descending on him and remaining with him. We can't understand the full significance of Jesus' confirmation by the Holy Spirit, but we do know that the presence of the Spirit gave Jesus the power to work miracles and the authority to speak God's truth.

Third confirmation: John the Baptist

The opening chapter of John's Gospel introduces the third confirming witness, John the Baptist:

> Then John gave this testimony: "I saw the Spirit come down from heaven as a dove and remain on him. And I myself did not know him, but the one who sent me to baptize with water told me, 'The man on whom you see the Spirit come down and remain is the one who will baptize with the Holy Spirit.' I have seen and I testify that this is God's Chosen One."[7]

As Jesus later said of John the Baptist, "You have sent to John and he has testified to the truth."[8] God gave John the Baptist the unique ministry and privilege of confirming the identity of Jesus, God's Chosen One and the Savior of the world.

Fourth confirmation: Jesus himself

In John's Gospel, Jesus takes the witness stand and testifies for himself. He acknowledges that a witness who offers only uncorroborated testimony cannot be trusted, which is why Jesus had other witnesses and evidence with which to back up his testimony.[9] After stating that he was confirmed by the witness of God the Father and John the Baptist, Jesus said, "I have testimony weightier than that of John. For the works that the Father has given me to finish—the very works that I am doing—testify that the Father has sent me."[10]

Jesus also said, "I and the Father are one."[11] Hearing this testimony, his opponents were enraged. They believed he had uttered blasphemy, claiming to be the Son of God and equal to God himself. So they picked up stones, intending to stone Jesus to death on the spot. "We are not stoning you for any good work," they said, "but for blasphemy, because you, a mere man, claim to be God."[12]

Jesus' testimony about himself would mean little if it were nothing but talk. But everything he did and said, from his miracles to his amazing wisdom, verified his claim. By his own testimony, backed up by solid evidence, Jesus confirmed that he was and is the Messiah, God's only Son, our Lord.

Fifth confirmation: Old Testament Scriptures

Inspired by the Holy Spirit, the Old Testament prophets foretold the birth, ministry, death, and resurrection of Jesus. Some of the most precise and unmistakable prophecies of

Jesus were recorded by the prophet Isaiah. He described Jesus' birth, his suffering, his role as a servant, and the ministry of John the Baptist, who announced him.[13]

When the corrupt religious leaders opposed Jesus, he told them, "You study the Scriptures diligently because you think that in them you have eternal life. These are the very Scriptures that testify about me, yet you refuse to come to me to have life."[14]

Sixth confirmation: Miracles

The Gospel of John calls the miracles of Jesus *signs*. The miracles John describes confirm the identity, purpose, and authority of Jesus as the Son of God. Jesus did not perform miracles in order to attract attention or draw crowds. In fact, many of his miracles (such as turning water into wine at Cana or the healing of the leper in Mark 1) were done quietly, away from public view. Often, he told those who had witnessed his miracles to tell no one. The fact that he performed many miracles without seeking attention and publicity confirms his statement to the religious leaders who opposed him: "I do not accept glory from human beings."[15]

Seventh confirmation: The disciples

The twelve disciples were with Jesus day and night throughout his three years of ministry on earth. They listened to his teachings, and they watched his life. If anyone could have spotted any sin, flaw, or hypocrisy in Jesus, it would have been those twelve men. When some of Jesus' followers found his teachings too difficult and turned away from him, the twelve remained. Asked whether the Twelve would also turn back from following him, Simon Peter, their spokesman, said, "Lord, to whom shall we go? You have the words of eternal life."[16]

John the son of Zebedee was one of those who continued to follow Jesus after many other followers defected. In the penultimate verse of John's Gospel, he writes, "This is the disciple who testifies to these things and who wrote them down. We know that his testimony is true."[17]

"Conceived by the Holy Spirit and Born of the Virgin Mary"

Every December, millions of people gather in churches to celebrate Christmas and commemorate the truth of the gospel. They sing carols of the Christian faith, and they declare that Jesus is our newborn King. But do they truly understand the significance of the carols they sing? Do they understand what it means that Jesus was conceived by the Holy Spirit and born of the Virgin Mary? Or does the profound meaning of Christmas go in one ear and out the other?

To a biblical, evangelical Christian, Christmas is not merely a sentimental, nostalgic holiday. It's the celebration of the incarnation of Jesus Christ, the Son of God. The first Christmas set in motion God's plan for the redemption of the human race. It was the ultimate expression of God's love for us. It was a unique and miraculous event that God initiated for our salvation and for his glory.

The arrival of the Savior of the world was promised in

the Garden of Eden.[18] The Savior was born to a young virgin named Mary. When God sent the angel Gabriel to tell Mary she was going to give birth to the Son of the Most High God, Mary asked, "How will this be, . . . since I am a virgin?"[19]

The angel replied, "The Holy Spirit will come on you, and the power of the Most High will overshadow you. So the holy one to be born will be called the Son of God."[20] Some people claim that it really doesn't matter whether Jesus was born of a virgin or not. They could not be more wrong. Why was it absolutely necessary that Mary was a virgin when she conceived Jesus? It's because only a virgin-born Savior could be free from original sin. Throughout the Old Testament, the perfect and sinless sacrifice of Jesus was symbolically represented by a lamb that was spotless and unblemished. That's why Peter called Jesus "a lamb without blemish or defect."[21]

Because Jesus was conceived by the Holy Spirit and born of the Virgin Mary, he was born perfect and sinless, as a sacrifice for sin must be. He was miraculously conceived, he lived a miraculously perfect life, and he was miraculously resurrected.

If we believe that God is God, that he is the Father almighty, the Creator of heaven and earth, then it's no problem for us to believe that Jesus could be conceived by the Holy Spirit and born of a virgin. It's no problem to believe in miracles. It's no problem to accept the authority of God's Word. If we do not believe in the Virgin Birth, then it's almost certain that we do not believe in God.

The Virgin Birth does not mean that God the Son came

into existence on that first Christmas. The Son has existed forever and was involved in the creation of heaven and earth. When God the Son took the form of a human baby, he didn't cease to be God. He became a man so that he could be the perfect, sinless sacrifice for our sin.

Evangelical theologian Wayne Grudem sums up the importance of the Virgin Birth this way: "God, in his wisdom, ordained a combination of human and divine influence in the birth of Christ, so that his full humanity would be evident to us from the fact of his ordinary human birth from a human mother, and his full deity would be evident from the fact of his conception in Mary's womb by the powerful work of the Holy Spirit."[22]

"Suffered under Pontius Pilate"

In John 18, the corrupt religious leaders bring Jesus to Pontius Pilate, the Roman governor of Judea, to be judged. The religious establishment had no authority to impose capital punishment. Only the Roman government could put Jesus to death. So the religious leaders accused Jesus of plotting rebellion against Caesar.

The dialogue between Jesus and Pilate is a tense, dramatic scene.

> Pilate . . . summoned Jesus and asked him, "Are you the king of the Jews?"
>
> "Is that your own idea," Jesus asked, "or did others talk to you about me?"

"Am I a Jew?" Pilate replied. "Your own people and chief priests handed you over to me. What is it you have done?"

Jesus said, "My kingdom is not of this world. If it were, my servants would fight to prevent my arrest by the Jewish leaders. But now my kingdom is from another place."

"You are a king, then!" said Pilate.

Jesus answered, "You say that I am a king. In fact, the reason I was born and came into the world is to testify to the truth. Everyone on the side of truth listens to me."

"What is truth?" retorted Pilate.[23]

Jesus must have pondered the grim irony of Pilate's question. Just hours earlier, in the upper room, he had said to his disciple Thomas, "I am the way and the truth and the life. No one comes to the Father except through me."[24]

After interrogating Jesus, Pilate concluded, "I find no basis for a charge against him."[25] He tried to release Jesus, but the crowd wouldn't let him. In the end, Pilate committed the cowardly act of having Jesus flogged and beaten, then tortured and executed on a Roman cross.

Jesus truly suffered under Pontius Pilate, and it undoubtedly saddens the heart of God to hear so many self-described "Christians" today echoing Pilate's question: "What is truth?"

Why is this line an important part of the Apostles' Creed? It's important because the judgment of Jesus by Pontius Pilate anchors the Crucifixion to a specific time and place in human history. Pilate was a real, historical figure whose words and deeds are recorded in secular history as well as in the Bible.

Because Jesus suffered under Pilate—enduring humiliation, physical agony, and emotional desolation under the lash of Pilate's soldiers—he understands our human condition, including our pain and suffering. He knows what it means to be unjustly accused. He knows what it means to be persecuted by enemies. He knows what it's like to be crushed and pierced and crucified without cause. Whatever you are going through right now, Jesus knows your suffering.

Because Jesus suffered under Pontius Pilate, the writer of Hebrews can say, "We do not have a high priest who is unable to empathize with our weaknesses, but we have one who has been tempted in every way, just as we are—yet he did not sin."[26]

"Was Crucified, Died, and Was Buried"

I have heard that some pastors and theologians have called the cross of Christ a negative message, a turn-off for unbelievers, and a hindrance to reaching the unchurched. Yet the early Christians counted it a privilege to identify themselves with the cross of Jesus Christ. They could have chosen any number of symbols to identify themselves as Christians. They could have chosen the star of Bethlehem to symbolize the Savior's birth, or the carpenter's bench to represent the profession of Jesus before he began his ministry, or the empty tomb to symbolize the Resurrection. They could have chosen the crucifix—the image of Jesus nailed to the cross. Instead, they chose to signify the Christian faith with the symbol of the empty cross.

The crucifix did not come into use until the sixth century. The first-century Christians chose the symbol of an empty cross because they wanted to announce to the world that the cross—and the tomb—are *empty*.

With the crucifixion of Jesus, God declared that the wages of sin had been paid in full. The perfect sinless sacrifice had been offered. Redemption was complete. Satan had pierced the heel of Jesus; but Jesus had crushed Satan's head, and the defeat of Satan was accomplished. The plan of God for the redemption of humanity was revealed.

In February 1923, J. Gresham Machen was invited to speak at the Moody Bible Institute Founder's Week Conference. Machen was one of the great defenders of the Bible against the apostate liberal "Christianity" of his day. In his address at the conference, he said that the atoning death of Christ is the basis of the Christian faith. Liberal preachers and theologians try to overcomplicate the meaning of atonement, he said, but it is really a very simple idea: "We deserve eternal death. The Lord Jesus Christ, because he loved us, died instead of us on the Cross."[27] Machen went on to say:

> That certainly is not incomprehensible. It is
> mysterious in its depth of grace, but it is a thing
> that a child can understand. Do you want me to
> tell you what is difficult? It is not the simple Bible

presentation of the death of Christ, but the manifold modern effort to get rid of that simple presentation of the cross in the interests of human pride.

The modern liberals pour out the vials of their scorn upon the Bible presentation of the Cross of Christ. They speak of it with disgust as involving a "trick" intended to placate an "alienated God." Thus they pour out their scorn upon a thing so holy that in the presence of it the Christian heart melts in gratitude too deep for words. . . .

The very nerve of the Christian view of the cross is that God Himself makes the sacrifice for our salvation. Where can love be found except at the Cross of Christ, the one who died, the just for the unjust? "For God so loved the world that he gave his only begotten son." There, and there alone, is to be found the love that is love indeed.[28]

With the death of Jesus, the Son, on the cross, God did not merely solve the sin problem. *He himself became the solution.*

"He Descended to Hell"

Understandably, this line of the Apostles' Creed is troubling to some evangelicals today. That's because there is a misunderstanding concerning the word *hell*. In Christian theology today, *hell* usually refers to the final place of eternal punishment.

But in the first century, when the Apostles' Creed was written, Christians used the term *hell* to refer to the grave or the abode of the dead, which they pictured as being located beneath the surface of the earth. In the ancient Latin version of the Creed, the word translated "hell" was *inferos*, which is related to our English word *inferior*. *Inferos* means "the inferior world" or "the underworld." This is the equivalent of what the Greeks called *Hades* and what the Jews called *Sheol*—the temporary abode of dead souls awaiting the final judgment. We see this concept in Paul's letter to the Ephesians:

> To each one of us grace has been given as Christ apportioned it. This is why it says:
>
>> "When he ascended on high,
>> he took many captives
>> and gave gifts to his people."
>
> (What does "he ascended" mean except that he also descended to the lower, earthly regions? He who descended is the very one who ascended higher than all the heavens, in order to fill the whole universe.)[29]

Jesus did not descend into a place of torment. He descended into the grave, the abode of the dead. He was crucified and he died. The Creed makes it clear that Jesus died, and he went to the place of the dead before being raised again on the third day.

"The Third Day He Rose Again from the Dead"

The Apostles' Creed tells us, "The third day he rose again from the dead." It's vitally important that we remember the resurrected Lord Jesus.

If Jesus had not risen from the dead on the third day, our civilization would not exist. Humanity would still be in the Dark Ages if not for the resurrection of Jesus. Christians—people who had placed their trust in the resurrected Lord Jesus—invented science, education, and modern medicine. Bible-believing Christians discovered the knowledge and created the institutions that made our modern world possible.

Christians who remembered the resurrection of Jesus invented our healthcare system. During the Middle Ages, Christian orders of monks, priests, and nuns founded the first hospitals in the world. The medieval French called a hospital a *hôtel Dieu*, or "hotel of God."

Christians who remembered the resurrection of Jesus invented universities. The first university was founded by Christians at Bologna, Italy, sometime around 1088. Christians founded Oxford in 1096. Christians founded the University of Paris around 1150. Bible-believing Christians invented higher education.

Christians who remembered the resurrection of Jesus invented the disciplines of science. Christian clerics believed that God had created an orderly world that could be studied and understood. Robert Grosseteste was bishop of Lincoln and an Oxford mathematician, responsible for helping to establish the scientific method of observation. Albertus Magnus, a German Dominican friar, wrote books on logic, chemistry, and astronomy. Jean Buridan was a French priest and one of the first true physicists; he studied the laws of inertia, momentum, and planetary motion.

Physicist Paul Davies observes, "The very notion of physical law is a theological one in the first place, a fact that makes many scientists squirm. Isaac Newton first got the idea of absolute, universal, perfect, immutable laws from the Christian doctrine that God created the world and ordered it in a rational way."[30]

All these advances in healthcare, higher education, and science came about because Jesus rose from the dead on the third day. Had there been no empty tomb, Christianity would be just another failed, dead religion. All the founders of all the other religions are dead, dead, dead. Because Jesus lives, Christianity lives. The resurrection of Jesus breathed life and the light of reason into our entire civilization.

Whatever you are facing right now, remember this all-important fact of history: On the third day, Jesus rose from the dead. If you are facing trials, sorrows, or disappointments, remember the resurrected Lord Jesus. The Resurrection will give you strength when you feel weak, victory when you feel defeated, comfort when you are sorrowing, and hope when you are in despair.

When Timothy was a struggling and discouraged young pastor in Ephesus, the apostle Paul wrote to him from a prison cell in Rome. His message was simple: "Remember

Jesus Christ, raised from the dead, descended from David. This is my gospel."[31] With those words, Paul encouraged his young protégé to remember the greatest event in all of human history—and to draw strength from it.

Remember the resurrected Jesus! Without the Resurrection, the Christian faith would be the greatest hoax in history and Christians would deserve nothing but pity.[32] But thanks be to God, Jesus is risen! He is risen indeed.

It's so easy to become bitter, discouraged, and angry in this life. It's so easy to become cynical and depressed. In times of disappointment, remember the resurrected Jesus. Resurrection power is a power the world does not understand.

For thousands of years, Old Testament prophets foretold the birth, ministry, death, and resurrection of Jesus Christ. As Paul said, "What I received I passed on to you as of first importance: that Christ died for our sins *according to the Scriptures*, that he was buried, that he was raised on the third day *according to the Scriptures*."[33]

From Genesis to Malachi, the Old Testament is brimming with prophecies about the Lord Jesus, including prophecies of the Resurrection. On the Day of Pentecost, Peter stood before a vast crowd in Jerusalem and preached the gospel:

Fellow Israelites, I can tell you confidently that the patriarch David died and was buried, and his tomb is here to this day. But he was a prophet and knew that God had promised him on oath that he would place one of his descendants on his throne. *Seeing what*

was to come, he spoke of the resurrection of the Messiah,
that he was not abandoned to the realm of the dead,
nor did his body see decay. God has raised this Jesus
to life, and we are all witnesses of it.[34]

What is the prophecy of David that Peter refers to? It is
Psalm 16:10, in which David, speaking for the Messiah while
addressing God the Father, writes, "You will not abandon
me to the realm of the dead, nor will you let your faithful
one see decay." Peter reasoned that because David died and
did see decay, he was writing not about himself but about
the Messiah. David wrote his prophecy of the Resurrection
a thousand years before Christ. Another Old Testament passage, Hosea 6:2, states, "After two days he will revive us;
on the third day he will restore us," a statement that many
theologians believe is a prediction of the resurrection of the
Messiah.

Remembering the resurrected Jesus will give you true and
lasting contentment. Life goes up and down, but you will be
comforted if you remember the resurrected Jesus. Problems
and crises will arise, but you will be reassured if you remember the resurrected Jesus. Illness and sorrows may strike at
you, but you will be encouraged if you remember the resurrected Jesus. You know that Jesus has gone through death,
and he is alive again. He has gone ahead of you to prepare a
place for you in heaven.

Your faith will be strong, unbreakable, invincible, as long
as you remember that, on the third day, Jesus rose again from
the dead.

"Ascended to Heaven . . . Seated at the Right Hand of God"

After Jesus was bodily resurrected from the dead, the Apostles' Creed instructs us, "He ascended to heaven and is seated at the right hand of God the Father almighty."

The Feast of the Ascension of Christ (sometimes called Ascension Day) commemorates the departure of Jesus into heaven. It is celebrated on a Thursday, forty days after Easter Sunday. On the first Ascension Day, Jesus rose into the heavenly realm. He visibly departed from the earth and entered heaven's gates, having completed his mission by securing a place in eternity for all who would call upon his name.

Though Ascension Day is largely ignored in the evangelical church today, it is a significant moment in history. Ascension Day emphasizes the authority of Jesus the Son:

> The Son is the radiance of God's glory and the exact representation of his being, sustaining all things by his powerful word. After he had provided purification for sins, he sat down at the right hand of the Majesty in heaven."[35]

Where is Jesus the Son right now? He is enthroned at the right hand of God the Father, exalted in glory. David prophesied that this would come to pass, as Peter declared in his Pentecost sermon:

> Exalted to the right hand of God, he has received from the Father the promised Holy Spirit and has

poured out what you now see and hear. For David did not ascend to heaven, and yet he said,

> "The Lord said to my Lord:
> 'Sit at my right hand
> until I make your enemies
> a footstool for your feet.'"

Therefore let all Israel be assured of this: God has made this Jesus, whom you crucified, both Lord and Messiah.[36]

Christ's position of authority in heaven affirms his identity as God incarnate, our only mediator, and *the only way* to the Father. Jesus was not just a good man; he was the perfect, sinless God-man. Jesus did not merely *teach* us about God; he *is* God. He did not merely *tell* us about salvation; he *is* our salvation. He did not merely *point* us to God; he *is* the only way to God.

Seated at the right hand of God the Father, Jesus' work as the great high priest and King of kings continues today. While we are going about our daily lives, while we are sleeping at night, Jesus is at the right hand of God, carrying out his Kingdom agenda for this fallen world. Even though the world does not recognize him, Jesus is already enthroned at the right hand of God the Father. A time is coming when every knee will bow before him, and every tongue will confess that Jesus Christ is Lord.

While we wait in this interval between the ascension of Christ and his return, we have a job to do, a commission to fulfill. We are to make disciples of all nations. We are to preach the gospel by the power of the Holy Spirit working in our lives.

Jesus said, "My Father's house has many rooms; if that were not so, would I have told you that I am going there to prepare a place for you? And if I go and prepare a place for you, I will come back and take you to be with me that you also may be where I am."[37] What a profound assurance! Jesus is preparing a place in heaven for you and me. His ascension continues to declare the gospel message of salvation by grace through faith.

Progressive "Christians," of course, criticize biblical, evangelical Christians for emphasizing heaven. As we have seen, one progressive leader even mocks biblical Christians for preaching a gospel that is "primarily information on how to go to heaven after you die."[38] This is hardly a new criticism. More than seventy years ago, C. S. Lewis grew weary of hearing people complain that Christians were so heavenly minded that they were of no earthly good. Writing in *Mere Christianity*, Lewis offered this insight:

> If you read history you will find that the Christians
> who did most for the present world were just
> those who thought most of the next. The Apostles
> themselves, who set on foot the conversion of the
> Roman Empire, the great men who built up the
> Middle Ages, the English Evangelicals who abolished
> the Slave Trade, all left their mark on Earth, precisely
> because their minds were occupied with Heaven. It

is since Christians have largely ceased to think of the other world that they have become so ineffective in this [one].[39]

If we keep our minds focused on our eternity with Jesus in heaven, we'll be amazed at all that God is able to accomplish through us here on earth.

"He Will Come to Judge"

Now that Jesus has risen from the dead, ascended to heaven, and is seated at the right hand of God the Father, the final line of the middle section of the Apostles' Creed tells us that "from there he will come to judge the living and the dead." This is a sobering statement. Judgment is coming. Am I ready to face the judgment of the Lord Jesus? Are *you* ready?

All religions are not the same. They don't all lead to the same destination. Did Buddha rise from the dead? Is Muhammad's tomb empty? Has Krishna walked out of his grave? No! Only Jesus has astonished the world by rising from the dead and by ascending to heaven in power and glory. Only Jesus guarantees our resurrection to eternal life.

When Jesus the Son returns, all who believe in him will have the great joy of being surprised by his love. And when he returns, all who rejected him will despair at his judgment.

Though the evidence for the Resurrection is overwhelming, we know that Satan has blinded the minds of unbelievers. When Jesus returns to judge the world, they will have to face his judgment without defense or excuse. The Resurrection established Jesus as the only one qualified to judge every human being who has ever lived. He is the only one who can save us from our sins and open the doorway to eternity.

Those who reject Jesus as Lord and Savior must face him as Judge. So you and I must ask ourselves, "When we stand before the courts of heaven, will we be able to say that we placed our entire faith in Jesus Christ, the crucified and risen Lord?"

If we can confidently answer *yes*, then we will be richly blessed by the third and final section of the Apostles' Creed.

I Believe in the Holy Spirit

For years early in my ministry, I avoided making media appearances. I refused to go on television. It wasn't that I was camera shy, but I had seen so many TV preachers, listened to so many radio preachers, and had heard the Scriptures distorted so grievously in electronic media that I simply wanted no part of it.

Over time, God showed me that he had work for me to do in electronic media. He opened doors for me to enter the world of radio and television, and I made my peace with the media. Today, *Leading The Way* broadcasts the uncompromised Word of God 13,000 times a week in 195 countries. This ministry can be received by nearly four billion people via satellite TV and other means, and God gets all the glory.

A few years ago, I was in a radio studio overseas. We were recording thirty radio messages in three days. My interpreter, Reverend Baki Sadaka, was in the studio with me. While recording, we ran into a technical problem. As we waited for the engineer to resolve the issue, Baki said, "Did you know, brother, that there are believers all around the world who pray for The Church of The Apostles on a daily basis? Wherever I go, people tell me, 'We watch The Church of The Apostles telecast every morning before we go to work, and we give thanks to God and pray for that ministry.'"

My heart was touched to realize that so many believers in poverty-stricken parts of the world are praying for our church in America. I'm reminded of how the poor believers in famine-plagued Jerusalem prayed for the church in rich, sin-plagued Corinth. Sometimes we who are rich in the West are tempted to think, *What can a poor believer do for me?* But whether rich or poor, whether in America or Africa or Asia or the Middle East, whether we live in freedom or under oppression and persecution, the words of the apostle Paul are still true: "We were all baptized by one Spirit so as to form one body—whether Jews or Gentiles, slave or free—and we were all given the one Spirit to drink."[1]

The Holy Spirit is our Advocate, Comforter, and Counselor, who indwells all genuine believers, uniting us in a common faith, compelled by the great commandment to love the Lord and love one another, sent out by the great commission to preach the gospel throughout the world.

Every genuine Christian should be able to affirm the closing section of the Apostles' Creed:

> I believe in the Holy Spirit,
> the holy catholic church,
> the communion of saints,
> the forgiveness of sins,
> the resurrection of the body,
> and the life everlasting. Amen.

While Jesus was on earth, he promised to send us the Holy Spirit. When he was with his disciples in the upper room, comforting them in the final hours before his death on the cross, he said, "I will ask the Father, and he will give you another advocate to help you and be with you forever."[2] Later that night, he told them, "When he, the Spirit of truth, comes, he will guide you into all the truth."[3]

After the Resurrection, and mere moments before he ascended into heaven, Jesus told the disciples, "You will receive power when the Holy Spirit comes on you; and you will be my witnesses in Jerusalem, and in all Judea and Samaria, and to the ends of the earth."[4]

All Christians today have access to the same Holy Spirit who was given to the believers in the first century. But do we really understand who the Holy Spirit is? In order to confidently affirm the statement "I believe in the Holy Spirit," we must think deeply about the person of the Holy Spirit and the work he does in our lives.

"I Believe in the Holy Spirit"

The Holy Spirit is the third person of the Trinity. The Spirit reveals God's truth and equips us to carry out the work of God's Kingdom. He guides us and empowers us to live holy and righteous lives. He quickens our dead spirit, transforms our fallen nature, and fills us with his empowering presence. He seals us so that we can never lose our salvation, once we come to an authentic saving faith in Christ.

> You also were included in Christ when you heard
> the message of truth, the gospel of your salvation.
> When you believed, you were marked in him with
> a seal, the promised Holy Spirit, who is a deposit
> guaranteeing our inheritance until the redemption
> of those who are God's possession—to the praise of
> his glory.[5]

We must not make the mistake of trivializing or under-valuing the power and role of the Holy Spirit. He is the breath of the living God. He is the hurricane force that created the universe. He is the breath of life that filled the lungs of the newly formed Adam. He is the mighty gale that parted the Red Sea.

When we were yet unconverted and worldly, dead in our sin and completely in denial of our need of a savior, the Holy Spirit opened our spiritual eyes and made us see that we were in rebellion against a holy God. He made us see that we were sinners, we were lost, and we could never save ourselves. The

Spirit showed us the way to repentance. The Spirit enabled us to understand the gospel and receive God's forgiveness through faith in Jesus. The Spirit raised us up from our spiritual grave and enabled us to be born again.

You may think that receiving Jesus as your Lord and Savior was your own idea. But if the Holy Spirit had not been speaking to your heart, urging you and drawing you to Jesus, you would still be lost in your sins. As Jesus said, "No one can come to me unless the Father who sent me draws them."[6] The Father draws us through the ministry of the Holy Spirit. God calls us by his grace, by his sovereign will, by his good pleasure, by his own mercy, and by his Spirit.

The Spirit leads us and guides us. He prompts us to do God's will, urging us to assist this person, pray for that person, and witness to yet another person. As we quiet our thoughts and focus on God in prayer, the Spirit is able to speak to us. The more mature we are in Christ, the better attuned we are to hear the quiet inner voice of the Holy Spirit.

Sometimes the Spirit urges us in one direction, and at other times the Spirit holds up a spiritual stop sign and says, "Don't go there." To our natural minds, the way ahead seems perfectly safe. But the Spirit can see all the pitfalls and hazards in our path, so he sometimes tells us to stop and go a different way. We see an example of this principle in Acts 16:6: "Paul and his companions traveled throughout the region of Phrygia and Galatia, having been kept by the Holy Spirit from preaching the word in the province of Asia." There was nothing wrong or sinful about Paul's plan to preach the gospel in Asia, but the Spirit of God had a better plan.

The Holy Spirit, who inspired the writing of the Word of God, will never contradict his Word. If you think you are being prompted to take a certain course of action, and that action would violate God's Word, then that inner prompting did *not* come from the Spirit. Some progressive "Christians" claim that the Spirit told them to preach a certain unbiblical doctrine or violate a biblical principle. I guarantee that prompting did *not* come from the Holy Spirit.

It takes time spent in the Scriptures and time spent in prayer to learn to hear the prompting of the Holy Spirit. God sees all of reality while we can see only a tiny piece of the puzzle. As a result, God's leadings and promptings sometimes don't make sense to us. At such times, we need to rely on God's leading, not our own human reason. As Proverbs 14:12 tells us, "There is a way that appears to be right, but in the end it leads to death." By learning to listen for the voice of the Spirit, we can avoid paths that lead to regret or even to death.

The Bible speaks in several places of the power of the Holy Spirit (see Luke 24:49; John 16:13; Acts 1:8; 2 Timothy 1:7; and 2 Peter 1:3). The word translated as "power" in our English Bible is the Greek word *dunamis*—meaning inherent power or energy—from which we get the word *dynamic*. The Holy Spirit provides the dynamic power to remove ungodliness from our lives. The Holy Spirit uses his power to break us so that he can then reshape us and remake us and conform us to the image and likeness of Christ.

To experience the power of the Holy Spirit, we must acknowledge our utter helplessness and complete dependence on God. The more we get our *self* out of the way and yield our will to his, the more of his power he can pour through us to better serve God and others. The power is his; we are only the conduits.

The Holy Spirit empowers us to share God's love even with people who are not humanly lovable. He empowers us to flee temptation. He empowers us to fight the good fight against our spiritual enemy, Satan. How, then, do we invite the power of the Holy Spirit to take over our lives?

We all know what it means to work and strive and strain to achieve success and promote ourselves. The key to spiritual power is the exact opposite of that kind of striving. The key to spiritual power is humility and brokenness. God delights in working through people with humble, broken spirits, people who are utterly dependent on him. The Spirit of God manifests his power in those who lay their weakness at his feet.

Someone once asked William Booth, founder of the Salvation Army, for the secret of the organization's success in transforming hearts and lives. Booth replied,

> I will tell you the secret. God has had all there was of me. There have been men with greater brains than I, men with greater opportunities. But from the day I got the poor of London on my heart and caught a vision of all Jesus Christ could do with them, on that day I made up my mind that God would have all of William Booth there was. And if there is anything of power in the Salvation Army today, it is because God

has had all the adoration of my heart, all the power of my will, and all the influence of my life.[7]

If we want to experience the power of the Holy Spirit to transform our lives and our world, we need to make ourselves completely available to the Spirit. You and I must let God have all there is of us—nothing held back.

We tend to focus on and pray for power. Instead, we must focus on the *source* of our power—the one who gives us the power to live righteous lives, the power to reach out to people in need, the power to proclaim the gospel with bold confidence, the power to love the unlovable and forgive the unforgivable. God wants us to be joyful Christians amid a wicked and hostile world. We can live joyful, righteous, effective lives only by relying on the power of the Holy Spirit.

The Spirit also opens our understanding of God's truth. The natural mind can't comprehend the things of God, so we need the enlightening power of the Holy Spirit to teach us God's truth. To the world, Jesus was just a good man, a great moral teacher, a role model of love and self-sacrifice. To the world, Jesus could not have been born of a virgin, could not have healed the sick and raised the dead, and could not have walked out of the tomb alive and resurrected. Only through the power of the Holy Spirit can we comprehend these great truths of the Christian faith.

By the power of the Holy Spirit, we understand that Jesus sits enthroned on the rim of the universe with authority and power. He is far above every name that is named, not only in this age but in the ages to come. He rules over powers, authorities, nations, dominions, kings, presidents, dictators, angels, devils, believers, and scoffers. He rules over his children and his church.

God assures us in his Word that it is no accident that we belong to him. He chose us and adopted us by the power of the Holy Spirit.

"The Holy Catholic Church, the Communion of Saints"

The Apostles' Creed moves from "I believe in the Holy Spirit" to "I believe in . . . the holy catholic church, [and] the communion of saints." There is a definite linkage between the Holy Spirit and the church.

At this point, we need to be very clear about the phrase *holy catholic church*. This is not a reference to Roman Catholicism. The word *catholic* (with a small *c*) means "comprehensive" or "universal." Thus the holy catholic church spoken of in the Apostles' Creed refers to all genuine believers, all true followers of Jesus Christ, from every denomination, in every era of history, all around the world.

The creed goes on to affirm a belief in "the communion of saints." This phrase refers to our unity with one another in the church of Jesus Christ. We share the same faith with all the saints who have gone before us. We share fellowship with all the saints in the church today. We share the same gospel, the same Word of God, the same access to God in prayer, the same sacraments of baptism and holy Communion, the same eternal life by grace through faith in Jesus Christ. In short, we have communion with God, communion with the saints above, and communion with one another in the church, the body of Christ.

The Christian faith was never meant to be lived in isolation. We need one another in the body of Christ. Involvement in the life of a local church is not an option for an authentic Christian. It is a requirement for a life of spiritual growth, health, and maturity.

We cannot adequately talk about the church of Jesus Christ and the communion of the saints without talking about spiritual gifts—the supernaturally endowed gifts that are given to individual Christians by the Holy Spirit. As the apostle Paul told the Ephesians:

> To each one of us grace has been given as Christ apportioned it. This is why it says:
>
> > "When he ascended on high,
> > he took many captives
> > and gave gifts to his people." . . .
>
> So Christ himself gave the apostles, the prophets, the evangelists, the pastors and teachers, to equip his people for works of service, so that the body of Christ may be built up until we all reach unity in the faith and in the knowledge of the Son of God and become mature, attaining to the whole measure of the fullness of Christ.[8]

In Ephesians 4, Paul lists five spiritual gifts: apostle, prophet, evangelist, pastor, and teacher. Romans 12:6-8 lists the spiritual gifts of prophecy, serving, teaching, encouragement, giving, leadership, and mercy. In 1 Corinthians 12:8-10, the list of gifts "given through the Spirit" includes a message of wisdom, a message of knowledge, faith, healing, miracles, prophecy, distinguishing between spirits, tongues, and interpretation of tongues. In 1 Corinthians 12:28-30 we find the gifts of apostle, prophet, teacher, miracles, healing, helps, guidance, and tongues. Peter also addresses spiritual gifts in 1 Peter 4:10-11. Some gifts were unique to that time, given to the newborn church to strengthen God's people during an era of rapid growth and intense persecution.

As Christians, we need to understand spiritual gifts and use them to build up the (small *c*) catholic church. The Holy Spirit has gifted you for service and ministry in the body of Christ. If you are not exercising the gifts the Spirit has given you, then you are not doing the good works you were created to do. God created us physically when we were conceived and born. He recreated us spiritually when we were born again, in order to accomplish his purpose for our lives. We glorify God when we exercise our spiritual gifts.

Suppose you gave me a birthday gift—and I *refused* it? Or perhaps I accepted it but set it on a shelf unopened. Or tossed it in the trash. Would you think I was uncaring and ungrateful? Would you feel hurt and brokenhearted? That is how many Christians treat the gifts God has given them through the Holy Spirit.

If you are a genuine follower of Christ, the Spirit has given at least one gift (and probably an array of gifts) to you. It's your "spiritual birthday gift" to celebrate your second birth. The Spirit custom-selected your gifts to match your uniqueness. God lavished great thought and care on you when he chose your gifts.

Each gift comes in many distinct varieties. For example, you may have the spiritual gift of teaching, as mentioned in Romans 12, 1 Corinthians 12, and Ephesians 4, but there are many kinds of teaching gifts. You may be especially gifted by God to teach adults or children, to teach simple gospel truths or complex philosophical concepts. You may teach a class of preschoolers or a university-level course in apologetics. If you gathered ten thousand people in one place, and they all had the spiritual gift of teaching, you'd find that no two would be exactly alike. We are all unique individuals, each with a unique pattern of spiritual gifts. Your pattern of spiritual gifting is your spiritual DNA.

God didn't shape us with a spiritual cookie cutter. In his sovereign plan, every individual believer is unique, one of a kind, and irreplaceable. If you don't use your gifts to do the work God has given you, that work won't get done. When we fail to use our gifts, we break the heart of the Giver, and we rob the body of Christ of the benefit of our gifts. All healthy bodies need exercise, and that includes the body of Christ. So exercise your gifts.

What will you do with the gifts the Holy Spirit has given you?

The Filling of the Spirit and the Fruit of the Spirit

The Holy Spirit *seals* us at the moment we surrender our lives to Christ. That is a once-for-all event. The Spirit guarantees that we belong to God, and our status with him will never change. His seal is certain, so our salvation is secure. We must only be sealed once. But what about the *filling* of the Holy Spirit?

"Be filled with the Spirit," Paul tells us in Ephesians 5:18, using a Greek verb tense that means to be constantly, continually filled. The filling of the Holy Spirit is an aspect of the Christian life that should take place regularly and continuously. Though every genuine Christian is sealed by the Holy Spirit, not every Christian chooses to be continuously filled by the Spirit. God waits for us to yield our will to his will. He will not come where he is not invited. Our joy and privilege is to invite the Holy Spirit to work in us and through us every day.

The filling of the Spirit takes place as we continually, prayerfully, moment by moment invite him to fill us and to direct our thoughts and words and actions. It means submitting every aspect of our lives to the Spirit's control. We cannot be filled with the Spirit unless we are 100 percent yielded to him. If you are holding back some dark, hidden corner of your life from God, he will not be able to guide you and use you through the filling of the Holy Spirit.

As we walk closely with the Lord, receiving our daily—even hourly—filling of the Holy Spirit, we will grow and become spiritually mature. We will begin to manifest what the Bible calls "the fruit of the Spirit." We find the fruit of the Spirit listed in Galatians 5:22-23: "The fruit of the Spirit is love, joy, peace, forbearance, kindness, goodness, faithfulness, gentleness and self-control. Against such things there is no law." The fruit of the Spirit is a pattern of character traits that we demonstrate as we become more and more mature in Christ.

Many people mistakenly refer to "the fruits of the Spirit," but the Bible speaks of this pattern of character traits as *one* fruit, not many fruits. Though the Holy Spirit may give us *some* spiritual *gifts* but not others, God wants to produce *all* the fruit of the Spirit in *each and every* Christian. The fruit of the Spirt is nothing less than the character and nature of God imparted to us.

The nature of God is characterized by love, joy, peace, forbearance, kindness, goodness, faithfulness, gentleness, and self-control. God's nature is not fragmented, and neither should our character be fragmented. If we tend to be impolite with others, we can ask the Spirit to help us grow in kindness. If we lack patience with others, we can ask the Spirit to help us grow in forbearance. If we are prone to anger or lust or overindulgence, we can ask the Spirit to help us grow in self-control. If we go around with a sour attitude, we can ask the Spirit to help us grow in joy.

Jesus said, "I am the vine; you are the branches. If you remain in me and I in you, you will bear much fruit; apart from me you can do nothing."[9] If we truly abide in Christ, if we are continually filled with the Spirit, we will bear *all* the fruit of the Spirit, not just some of it.

Forgiveness, Resurrection, and Life Everlasting

The Apostles' Creed concludes with this statement: "I believe in . . . the forgiveness of sins, the resurrection of the body, and the life everlasting. Amen." Many "Christians" today no longer affirm that statement. In place of forgiveness of sins, they offer tolerance of sins. In place of a coming bodily resurrection and life everlasting, they offer a social and political "kingdom" of the here and now.

The spirit of the age in which we live is a spirit of moral relativism, which manifests in a reluctance to say that sin is sin. The spirit of the age says that God does not care about morality and righteous behavior. The spirit of the age says that God loves us too much to judge us for our sin. The spirit of the age stands in opposition to the moral teachings of the Word of God.

Romans 6:23 tells us that "the wages of sin is death." Sin has a price, and that price is *death*. Any sin we commit ushers in death and decay to our lives. Sexual immorality kills intimacy. Lying slays integrity. Gossip destroys relationships. Every sin brings death into our lives. The spirit of the age declares that God is soft on sin. Not true! Sin is costly. Sin is deadly. God hates sin because he is holy, he is just, and he loves us.

Though Romans 6:23 begins by telling us "the wages of sin is death," it triumphantly concludes with this declaration: "The gift of God is eternal life in Christ Jesus our Lord." That is good news! There is forgiveness of sins, there is a resurrection of the body, and there is life everlasting. Amen! God loves us too much to abandon us to sin and death. He sent his Son, Jesus, to pay the wages of our sin and to set us free from death. He offers this freedom to everyone who will come to him.

This is the Good News we preach: God, the Father almighty, sent his Son to die in our place so that we can have the forgiveness of sins, the resurrection of the body, and the life everlasting. His love can set the captives free. His power can liberate us from the tyranny of sin, shame, and addiction. He is the one who heals and restores.

Are you sharing this Good News with everyone around you? Do you have friends who don't take sin seriously, who don't take their eternal destiny seriously? Do you pray for them? Do you talk to them? Do you agonize over their lost condition and their separation from God?

The spirit of the age would have us believe that all spiritual paths lead to the same destination—that we don't need to worry about the eternal destiny of our friends and loved ones. That we don't have to worry about sin and moral behavior. The deceptive, destructive spirit of the age would have us believe that God will simply wink at our sins and let everyone into heaven regardless.

But for two thousand years, faithful, Bible-believing Christians have said "no!" to the lying spirit of the age. They have stood firm on the great confession of our faith articulated in the Apostles' Creed:

I believe in God, the Father almighty,
Creator of heaven and earth.

I believe in Jesus Christ, his only Son, our Lord,
who was conceived by the Holy Spirit
and born of the virgin Mary.
He suffered under Pontius Pilate,
was crucified, died, and was buried;
he descended to hell.
The third day he rose again from the dead.
He ascended to heaven
and is seated at the right hand of God the Father
almighty.
From there he will come to judge the living and the
dead.

I believe in the Holy Spirit,
the holy catholic church,
the communion of saints,
the forgiveness of sins,
the resurrection of the body,
and the life everlasting. Amen.

✝

PART THREE

GRACE
AND TRUTH
TOGETHER

Living Out an Uncompromised Faith

A few years after The Church of The Apostles was founded, the pastor of a very large and thriving congregation visited us. He sat in on one of our services and listened to me preach. Later, in a private conversation, he told me that our church would never grow if I continued to preach in such an uncompromising, in-your-face way. If I wanted to have a large church ministry that would have an impact on our community, he said, I should keep my sermons positive and happy. There were certain passages of Scripture, he said, that I should not preach from.

I understood what this pastor was telling me, and I know he believed he was giving me helpful advice. I will be quite candid with you: I considered his advice and wondered,

What if he's right? But I didn't wonder for very long. I soon felt an inner prompting of the Lord, saying to me, "Michael, I would rather you arrive in heaven with a handful of people who came to a saving faith through your uncompromised preaching than have you entertain tens of thousands who will curse you from hell because you compromised my truth."

That moment, when I felt a strong sense of conviction from the Lord, was a turning point in my ministry. From that day forward, I made a point of preaching the uncompromised gospel of Jesus Christ. In fact, "Passionately Proclaiming Uncompromising Truth" became the motto of our global ministry, Leading The Way. We also adopted the following mission statement for our church:

Reaching the Lost and Equipping the Saints for the Work of Ministry. We are an evangelical congregation, declaring the whole counsel of God, as evidenced through our Statement of Faith. Nothing we do is as important as following Jesus' words in Matthew 24:14: "This Gospel of the Kingdom will be preached in the whole world as a testimony to all nations."

Ever since I felt the Lord call me to preach an uncompromised gospel, our church has grown and grown. From a tiny congregation of forty adults, we have grown to a large congregation with a media outreach that stretches around the globe. God always honors his uncompromised Word.

We joyfully celebrate God's truth at The Church of The

Apostles, but we do not shy away from the hard truths and challenging statements of God's Word. We understand that if we preach the uncompromised Word of God, people will accuse us of being negative and intolerant. The world doesn't understand that Christians can love sinners while condemning sin—just as God does.

Love compels and motivates us to share the crucified and resurrected Christ with everyone. Love compelled and motivated me to write this book and to reach out to leaders and teachers who claim to be Christians but have compromised God's truth. Sometimes, love will make us sound intolerant. I could win many friends in the world if I would simply compromise God's truth. But I love people and God's Word too much to watch people depart from the faith without urging them to repent.

The late Adrian Rogers summed it up well when he said:

It is better to be divided by truth than to be united in error. It is better to speak the truth that hurts and then heals, than falsehood that comforts and then kills. Let me tell you something, friend, it is not love and it is not friendship if we fail to declare the whole counsel of God. It is better to be hated for telling the truth, than to be loved for telling a lie. It is impossible to find anyone in the Bible who was a power for God who did not have enemies and was not hated. It's better to stand alone with the truth, than to be wrong with a multitude. It is better to ultimately succeed with the truth than to temporarily succeed with a lie. There is only one gospel, and Paul said, "If any man preach any other gospel unto you than that which we have preached unto you, let him be accursed."[1]

Jesus, in his upper-room prayer before going to the cross, prayed not only for his first-century followers, but also for his twenty-first-century followers—that is, for you and me:

> My prayer is not for them alone. I pray also for those who will believe in me through their message, that all of them may be one, Father, just as you are in me and I am in you. May they also be in us so that the world may believe that you have sent me. I have given them the glory that you gave me, that they may be one as we are one—I in them and you in me—so that they may be brought to complete unity. Then the world will know that you sent me and have loved them even as you have loved me.[2]

Jesus said that *unity* is our witness to the world. Our witness is hindered and diminished when we divide into factions of left and right, when we preach two disconnected gospels—a gospel of repentance, faith, salvation, and eternal life versus a "gospel" of progressive social and political activism that seeks to make Christianity more "palatable" and "acceptable" in our culture. We cannot "save" Christianity by dismembering its core truths.

I wish to open a respectful dialogue with those who have

wandered from biblical faith by altering and exchanging the truth of God's Word for a "more affirming" alternative. One of my concerns is that the evangelical church is being tempted to follow progressive "Christians" down this path.

In recent years, a well-known evangelical pastor has advocated that we Christians should eliminate the Old Testament from our presentation of the gospel and base our apologetics first and foremost on the resurrection of Jesus. Though he still affirms that the entire Bible is inspired by God, he's come to believe that the violence and miracles in the Old Testament are a stumbling block for some in our culture, and we should remove that obstacle to faith. He says he was motivated to rethink how he presents the gospel and its relationship to the Old Testament after hearing a scathing critique of the Bible by atheist spokesman Sam Harris. He was also persuaded by hearing several "deconversion" stories—anecdotal accounts of people who had left the church after losing faith in the reliability of Scripture.

I would not put this pastor in the same category as the progressive "Christians" who have abandoned belief in the Bible as the inspired Word of God. Still, I don't understand why he thinks that people whose faith is upset by Old Testament miracles will find New Testament miracles any more palatable—including the miracle of the Resurrection. That's the slippery slope that is already leading some evangelicals toward the same place of unbelief that the progressives occupy.

Those who "deconvert" today are no different from those disciples who defected from Jesus in John 6. After witnessing the feeding of the five thousand and hearing Jesus explain—based on Moses and the Prophets—that he was the "bread of life," the "bread from heaven,"[3] they said to Jesus, "This is a hard teaching. Who can accept it?"[4] As a result, John tells us, "many of his disciples turned back and no longer followed him."[5] What was the "hard teaching" they couldn't accept? From the Old Testament, Jesus established his credentials as the Messiah—and as a result, many of his disciples decided to "deconvert."

How did Jesus respond? Did he stop preaching from the Old Testament Scriptures? No, he continued to teach and preach from the authoritative Word of God. John tells us that "Jesus had known from the beginning which of them did not believe and who would betray him."[6] And this is why Jesus said, "No one can come to me unless the Father has enabled them.'"[7]

When people "deconvert" today, it's not because the Old Testament is full of errors, or too much violence, or miracles that are just too implausible to swallow. When people appear to deconvert, it's because God the Father didn't enable them to believe. That's straight from the lips of Jesus.

Another part of this pastor's argument is that Christianity began with the Resurrection, not with the Bible. Actually, a stronger case can be made that Christianity began in Genesis 3:15, when God told the serpent in Eden that a descendant of Eve (that is, Jesus) would crush the serpent's head, and the serpent would strike Jesus' heel. That was the first promise of the coming Messiah, and from that point on, Old Testament promises became increasingly numerous, specific, and compelling until they reached their fulfillment in the Gospels.

The Bible is one continuous story that peaks with the Resurrection and culminates in the second coming of the risen Christ. As Jesus himself said, "You study the Scriptures diligently because you think that in them you have eternal life. These are the very Scriptures that testify about me."[8] The Old Testament is a rich source of proofs of Jesus's identity as the Messiah. Why would any minister of the gospel want to abandon that gold mine?

One of the most exciting proofs that Jesus is the Messiah is found in the Old Testament book of Daniel. There, the angel Gabriel told Daniel, "Know and understand this: From the time the word goes out to restore and rebuild Jerusalem until the Anointed One, the ruler, comes, there will be seven 'sevens,' and sixty-two 'sevens.'"[9] Though Daniel himself probably didn't understand the meaning of the seven sevens and the sixty-two sevens, we now know that Gabriel gave Daniel a precise timetable for the arrival of the long-promised Messiah—"the Anointed One."

When Gabriel gave Daniel that prophecy, Israel was in exile in Persian-controlled Babylon. Gabriel was telling Daniel—and us—that a proclamation would be issued, ordering the reconstruction of Jerusalem. Following that decree, seven sevens of years plus sixty-two sevens of years would pass, and then the Messiah, the Anointed One, would appear.

A few years ago, attorney Frederick A. Larson studied this prophecy, updating an inquiry into Gabriel's prophecy by Scotland Yard official Sir Robert Anderson in his 1881 book, *The Coming Prince*. Larson began with the assumption that the "sevens" in Gabriel's prophecy are seven-year periods, and he performed a simple calculation: 7 times 7 equals 49; 62 times 7 equals 434; 49 plus 434 equals 483. So the Messiah would come to Israel 483 years after the decree to rebuild Jerusalem. Larson knew that the people of that era used a 360-day calendar, so 483 biblical years equals 476 years on our calendar.

When was the decree to rebuild Jerusalem issued? Larson explained, "The prophet Nehemiah records such a decree, and he dates it as the twentieth year of Artaxerxes. On our calendar, that date is 444 BC"[10] Larson determined that the Messiah's time would come in the year AD 33, according to Gabriel's prophecy.

Jesus made his triumphant entry into Jerusalem on a Sunday, and he was crucified the following Friday. Larson knew that the Crucifixion had to have occurred in a year when the 14th of Nisan fell on a Friday. The 14th of Nisan fell on a Friday only twice during Pilate's time as procurator: April 7, AD 30, and April 3, AD 33. It quickly becomes clear that Friday, April 3, AD 33, was the date of the Crucifixion. The Lord's triumphal entry into Jerusalem—the official appearance of the Messiah to Israel—took place on Sunday, March 29, AD 33—exactly as Gabriel foretold.

Bible scholars estimate that more than three hundred prophecies concerning the Messiah, like this one, are woven throughout the Old Testament. They predict the birth, ministry, suffering, death, resurrection, and triumphant return of the Messiah. As Jesus told his followers and his opponents, all these prophecies pointed directly to him and to no one else. So to suggest that we base what we say about Jesus on the event of the Resurrection alone, without anchoring our appeal in the amazingly accurate prophecies and proofs found in the Old Testament, is simply a wrong-minded approach. It's hard to imagine a more tragic message for the church.

After all, the Old Testament prophecies were not given primarily for the people of the Old Testament. The people in Old Testament times couldn't even understand them. Gabriel's prophecy was a complete mystery until Sir Robert Anderson did the math in the late nineteenth century, and Frederick Larson refined the calculations a few years ago. So who was Gabriel's prophecy for? It was for *us*—today!

The great English astronomer and mathematician Sir Isaac Newton (1643–1727) explained, "[God] gave this and the Prophecies of the Old Testament, not to gratify men's curiosities, by enabling them to foreknow things, but that, after that they were fulfilled, they might be interpreted by the event, and his own providence, not the interpreter's, be then manifested thereby to the world. For the event of things, predicted many ages before, will then be a convincing argument that the world is governed by providence."[11]

The entire Bible, Old Testament and New, was given for us today. If people in our day and age have a problem accepting it, the answer is not to downplay the Old Testament and assert that Christianity and the Bible began on the Resurrection day. The answer is that we need to do a better job of teaching the full counsel of God, beginning at Genesis and continuing through Revelation. We need to do a better job of presenting the entire Bible as a consistent whole, the story of Jesus the Messiah, from that first glimmer of a promise in Genesis 3:15, through his amazing life, death, and resurrection in the Gospels, to his eventual return, predicted throughout the New Testament. We must proclaim the truth about Jesus—the whole truth and nothing but the truth.

I'm amazed at the willingness of some preachers today to veer away from a traditional and biblical understanding of the Christian faith. Jesus didn't change what he taught in order to appeal to those who couldn't accept his "hard teachings." We must not do that either. There are disturbing warnings in God's Word against misleading the faithful and causing believers to stumble. The apostle James writes, "Not many of you should become teachers, my fellow believers, because you know that we who teach will be judged more strictly."[12] Those who have come up with some bold new spin on Christianity should be especially nervous.

I have never wanted to write or preach some "new" or "original" take on Christianity. There's nothing I preach that you haven't heard before. When I teach and preach and write, my goal is to remind my hearers of the old truths they've heard before but perhaps have forgotten. Very few "new" interpretations of the Bible are all that new anyway. There's nothing new under the sun. Most "new" interpretations are merely variations on some ancient heresy. Wanting to give people a new version of Christianity can take you into dangerous territory. It can lead to apostasy and unbelief—and if you are a leader or a pastor, you can take a lot of people into error with you.

A Fountain of Tears

In Numbers 13–14, Moses sends twelve spies into the land of Canaan as scouts, prior to Israel's entrance into the land. God has already promised them the land of Canaan. All they have to do is walk in and take it. But when the twelve spies return with their report, they are divided. Ten spies give the majority report: "We can't attack those people; they are stronger than we are. . . . The land we explored devours those living in it. All the people we saw there are of great size."[13]

But two spies, Joshua and Caleb, delivered the minority report: "The land we passed through and explored is exceedingly good. If the Lord is pleased with us, he will lead us into that land, a land flowing with milk and honey, and will give it to us. Only do not rebel against the Lord. And do not be afraid of the people of the land, because we will devour them. Their protection is gone, but the Lord is with us. Do not be afraid of them."[14]

Tragically, the cowardly majority won. Fear prevailed over faith. Even though the ten spies had seen the hand of God deliver them miraculously from Egypt, even though they had seen the plagues and the parting of the Red Sea and the drowning of the mighty Egyptian army, they were afraid of the Canaanites. They responded with unbelief and apostasy. So God decreed that only the faithful would enter the Promised Land—and that included Joshua and Caleb. Everyone else who retreated in unbelief was condemned to wander in the wilderness for forty years and die without ever reaching the Promised Land.

To me, those who abandon certain passages of God's Word are like the spies who refused to believe God's promise and boldly enter the Promised Land. There is always a price to pay for turning our backs on God's Word. If you are saved, you won't lose your salvation, but you will miss out on the blessings that are promised to those who hold fast to the teachings of God's Word.

My heart grieves over the current condition of the church of Jesus Christ. I don't mean for these words to seem judgmental or harsh. Instead, I am sorrowful over the kinds of teachings I have catalogued in this book. It hurts me deeply to say these things.

But I am convinced that God is sounding an alarm across this land, in the hope of awakening the church of Jesus Christ from its spiritual apathy and its neglect of biblical truth. God is calling us to take a bold, uncompromising, unashamed stand for the gospel of Jesus Christ and for every word of the Bible, both Old Testament and New.

The prophet Jeremiah preached for forty years, trying to persuade the people of Judah to repent of their apostasy and idolatry—but to no avail. Not a single person in Judah listened to him. Not a single person repented, even though he warned that God's judgment would certainly fall upon that unrepentant nation. I empathize and identify with the anguished words of Jeremiah when he writes:

Oh, that my head were a spring of water
and my eyes a fountain of tears!

I would weep day and night
    for the slain of my people.[15]

In Jeremiah's day, God's own people had turned away from the demands of the faith that God had entrusted to the nation. The preachers in Jeremiah's days were telling the people they had nothing to worry about, that God was tolerant of their idolatry, that he would never judge the nation. They preached a false gospel of inclusion and universalism: that it was perfectly fine with God if the people also worshiped and sacrificed to the demonic gods and goddesses of the surrounding culture. While Jeremiah preached judgment and conviction and repentance, the priests of Judah kept the crowd happy, entertained, and apathetic.

Jeremiah, a lone voice of uncompromised truth, warned the people until his voice was hoarse and he was blue in the face. He told them that judgment was coming, the Babylonians were on their way, and God would use that godless nation as his instrument of judgment. Jeremiah wept fountains of tears for his people.

How did the people respond? They tried to kill him by throwing him into a cistern full of mud.[16]

If God is God, then judgment awaits the church. Look at the state of our society. Look at the state of moral disarray our nation is in. Yes, we may blame the political parties or the Supreme Court or the news media or the entertainment media for all the immorality and injustice in our nation, but that's just the world being the world. If we are honest with ourselves, we must acknowledge that the moral decline in our culture is our fault—the fault of the church. As the church goes, so goes society.

Preacher after preacher, church after church, denomination after denomination—Christians are selling their spiritual birthright. So-called evangelicals have become ashamed of the *evangelium*, the Good News of Jesus Christ. They have sought friendship with the world, acceptance by the world, and praise from the world, and they have mutilated the Bible and diluted the gospel in the process. Instead of faith and boldness, they prize uncertainty, thinking that they are somehow "saving Christianity." But as the apostle Paul writes, "If the trumpet does not sound a clear call, who will get ready for battle?"[17]

These would-be saviors have exchanged prayer for marketing strategies, salvation for social action, holiness for happiness, power from God for favor with men, and timeless truths for clever lies. They have focused on what is profitable at the expense of what is prophetic. They have settled for what sells instead of the one who saves.

"Oh, that my head were a spring of water and my eyes a fountain of tears!"

Speaking the Truth in Love

The Christians of the first-century church refused to compromise the truth of the gospel. Because of their principled stand for the truth, some were fed to hungry lions, some were immersed in boiling oil, some were coated in tar and ignited as blazing torches in Nero's garden. Why did they refuse to recant their faith, even under the threat of torture and death? It's because they were determined to deliver a pure and uncompromised faith to future generations, including to you and me.

The faith that we have received from previous generations is a trust, and we must be faithful trustees of the Christian message. We must hand it down to future generations uncompromised, unmodified, and undefiled.

In Galatians 6:1, the apostle Paul gives us a principle for confronting those who stray from the truth. We who live by the Spirit should talk to that person, speaking God's truth while gently urging that person to repent. "But," Paul adds, "watch yourselves, or you also may be tempted."

The temptation to defect from the faith is a serious threat to our souls. It is so easy to rationalize falsehood and to compromise with the world. It's so easy to selectively quote only our favorite Scripture passages. Before we know it, we have fallen away from the faith. We find ourselves thinking worldly thoughts and viewing the Bible as a series of metaphors instead of God's revealed truth. We find ourselves rationalizing sin in ourselves and others. Eager to be accepted and approved by our worldly friends, desperate to avoid being ostracized for our politically incorrect views, we compromise and defect.

We must never be afraid to confront false teaching. In reliance on the Holy Spirit, we must confidently and boldly uphold the truth of the Bible. In Ephesians 4:11-15, Paul says:

Christ himself gave the apostles, the prophets, the evangelists, the pastors and teachers, to equip his people for works of service, so that the body of Christ may be built up until we all reach unity in the faith and in the knowledge of the Son of God and become mature, attaining to the whole measure of the fullness of Christ.

Then we will no longer be infants, tossed back and forth by the waves, and blown here and there by every wind of teaching and by the cunning and craftiness of people in their deceitful scheming. Instead, speaking the truth in love, we will grow to become in every respect the mature body of him who is the head, that is, Christ.

So we must speak the truth, but we must always speak the truth *in love*. We must speak rationally, reasonably, with hearts full of love for those who are teaching falsehood. Don't expect to be loved in return. Often, in their attempts to intimidate and silence us, apostates will accuse us of being unloving and even hateful. It is loving—they say—to let sinning people continue in their sin. It's hateful and intolerant—they say—to confront sin.

Their idea of love is not God's idea of love. To defectors from the faith, love means capitulating to sin. Love means compromising with sin. Love means silencing the truth.

But God says that if we love people, we speak the truth—gently but firmly. If we love people, we confront sin. If we love people, we warn them of the danger of error. If we love people, we hold fast to God's Word and to all of the teachings of the Lord Jesus, and we contend for the faith that was once for all entrusted to God's holy people.

In the words of the apostle John, "The Word became flesh and made his dwelling among us. We have seen his glory, the glory of the one and only Son, who came from the Father, full of grace and truth."[18] We see both the grace of Jesus and the truth of Jesus in action in John 8, when he deals with the woman caught in adultery. When none of the woman's accusers dares to cast the first stone, Jesus tells her, "Neither do I condemn you."[19] That's grace! The woman had sinned— but Jesus had removed her condemnation.

The progressive "Christians" would end the story on that note of grace. Progressive "Christianity" is long on grace but short on truth.

But because Jesus is full of grace *and* truth, he continues, "Go now and leave your life of sin."[20] That's truth. Grace without truth is weak on sin. Truth without grace is harsh and punishing. But grace and truth together provide the perfectly balanced, restorative, Christlike solution to sin. Jesus spoke the truth in love, and so should we.

God is for sinners, but God is against sin. In fact, one of the reasons God hates sin so much is that he loves sinners so much—too much to leave them drowning in their sin. God is for sinners who are caught in adultery, but God is against adultery. God is for sinners caught in homosexuality, but God is against homosexual sin. That is grace and truth.

Homosexuality is not a worse abomination than adultery or idolatry or other forms of immorality. It's on the same plane with other sins Paul wrote about: "Do you not know that wrongdoers will not inherit the kingdom of God? Do not be deceived: Neither the sexually immoral nor idolaters nor adulterers nor men who have sex with men."[21]

The solution to sin is not to repeal God's condemnation of sin in the Bible. The solution to sin is to welcome sinners while teaching God's uncompromised truth about sin. Authentic Christians do not hate LGBTQ people. We love them with the love of Jesus. We do not embrace the secular LGBTQ political agenda, but we embrace sinners of every kind, because we all are sinners and we have no moral right to look down on anyone. We believe that the sin problem was solved on the cross of Jesus Christ, and the ground is level at the foot of the cross.

Gay-pride activists don't represent all people with same-sex attraction issues. Many people struggle valiantly with temptations that arise from their sexual identity and sexual confusion. Many people with homosexual or bisexual tendencies live celibate lives, just as many single heterosexual people choose to live celibate lives.

The fact that we believe and preach God's uncompromised Word does not mean we are haters or bigots or homophobes. It means we respect the authority of Scripture and refuse to allow any secular social or political agenda to take precedence over faithfulness to God's Word.

As a Christian and a minister of the Word, I have always tried to befriend people who are in the gay or lesbian lifestyle. In the high-rise building where I have offices, I have gay neighbors and I always greet them when I see them in the hall. They know that I'm an evangelical Christian pastor, and they often seem wary of me. But I continue to greet them with the welcoming, accepting love of Christ, as I would do with anyone.

How do we live out our uncompromised faith? We live out the truth with grace, and we confidently, unashamedly speak the truth in love.

"That Born Again Thing"

In his book *The Irresistible Revolution*, progressive speaker and activist Shane Claiborne recalls a chapel service when he attended Wheaton College. The speaker was contemporary Christian singer Rich Mullins, the writer of such beloved worship songs as "Awesome God" and "Step by Step." Claiborne quotes Mullins as saying,

> You guys are all into that born again thing, which is great. We do need to be born again, since Jesus said that to a guy named Nicodemus. But if you tell me I have to be born again to enter the kingdom of God, I can tell you that you have to sell everything you have and give it to the poor, because Jesus said

that to one guy too. . . . But I guess that's why God invented highlighters, so we can highlight the parts we like and ignore the rest.[1]

This statement misses the point of the story of Jesus and the rich young ruler in Mark 10:17-23. In that account, a wealthy young man runs up to Jesus and says, "Good teacher, what must I do to inherit eternal life?" And Jesus tells him that he must keep all the Ten Commandments. The young man says, "All these I have kept since I was a boy."

Of course, no one can keep *all* the Ten Commandments perfectly, but Jesus didn't argue that point. He was trying to get to a more urgent issue in the young man's life. The text tells us that Jesus "looked at him and loved him." I think Jesus saw a real sincerity of heart in him; but there was something in the young man's soul that was a roadblock to his salvation.

"One thing you lack," Jesus said. "Go, sell everything you have and give to the poor, and you will have treasure in heaven. Then come, follow me."

The young man walked away sad, Mark tells us, "because he had great wealth."

Now, was Jesus saying that the way to be saved and have eternal life is to sell everything you have and give it to the poor? If you read the story carefully, it's clear that Jesus was not saying that at all. He gave the same plan of salvation to the rich young ruler that he gave to Nicodemus—but he gave it in different words, and he tailored his presentation of the gospel to each man's individual need.

Nicodemus was a Pharisee, and he had certain rigid, legalistic ideas about what it meant to be saved by God. Jesus had to shake him out of his narrow mind-set by telling him he needed to be born again. Likewise, Jesus knew that the rich young ruler's heart was tightly gripped by all his possessions, so he tried to shake the materialism out of the young man's heart by telling him to sell everything and give to the poor. The point of the story was *not* that giving to the poor would save his soul, but that his love of possessions prevented him from following Jesus.

The Bible is unambiguous on this point: Good works won't save you. Only Jesus saves. By grace are you saved through faith. Salvation is a gift of God, not an achievement of our own works. The plan of salvation that Jesus gave to Nicodemus was the same plan of salvation he gave the rich young ruler. He told Nicodemus that whosoever believes in him will have everlasting life. He told the rich young ruler, "Follow me." Believing in Jesus and following Jesus are the same thing.

When Jesus called Peter and Andrew, he didn't tell them to sell their fishing boats and give the money to the poor. He simply said, "Come, follow me."[2] Jesus dealt differently with each person he met, because he treated each one as a unique individual. But no matter who he was talking to, the plan of salvation he shared was the same: believe and follow Jesus.

For many years, evangelists and preachers have used terms like "receive Christ" or "invite Jesus into your heart" to describe Christian conversion. The decision to receive Christ is always accompanied by a prayer of commitment. In his book *Love Wins*, Rob Bell ridicules the idea of a conversion prayer:

> Christians don't agree on exactly what this prayer is, but for many the essential idea is that the only way to get into heaven is to pray at some point in your life, asking God to forgive you and telling God that you accept Jesus, you believe Jesus died on the cross to pay the price for your sins, and you want to go to heaven when you die. Some call this "accepting Christ," others call it the "sinner's prayer," and still others call it "getting saved," being "born again," or being "converted."
>
> That, of course, raises more questions. What about people who have said some form of "the prayer" at some point in their life, but it means nothing to them today? What about those who said it in a highly emotionally charged environment like a youth camp or church service because it was the thing to do, but were unaware of the significance of what they were doing? What about people who have never said the prayer and don't claim to be Christians, but live a more Christlike life than some Christians?[3]

Here is someone who founded a church and was a pastor for thirteen years, yet he seems to have completely missed the point of the prayer of conversion. Obviously, praying a prayer at one point in your life does not make you a follower of Christ. Charles Templeton prayed that prayer. Michael Shermer prayed that prayer. Both became world-famous advocates for atheism. Jesus did not say to Nicodemus and the rich young ruler, "One thing you lack—just pray the sinner's prayer." No! He said, "Believe in me. Follow me."

Praying to receive Christ as your Lord and Savior is not a magical incantation or a spiritual prescription. It's a commitment to follow Jesus and make him the Lord of your entire life. If it's a decision you make lightly or in an emotional moment, and you do not keep that commitment, then you were never saved to begin with.

Conversion is not a matter of praying the right words. Conversion is a matter of believing and following Jesus. It means not merely receiving him as your Savior but making him the Lord of your life. For some people, following Christ begins by praying a prayer. For others, the decision to follow Jesus takes place gradually, and they have no recollection of a single moment when they prayed to accept Christ. That's okay. What really matters is believing and following Christ.

So yes, as Rich Mullins said, I'm "into that born again thing." Jesus said we must be born again. He said we must follow him. And if we all follow him as our Savior and Lord, if we abide in him and hold to his teachings, our lives—and our world—will be transformed. So I hope and pray that you're also "into that born again thing."

I hope you'll take some time to examine your life and your soul, and ask yourself, "Do I truly believe in Jesus? Am I following him? Have I made him the Lord of my life?" If your honest, searching answer to those questions is *yes*, then take a moment to thank Jesus for dying on the cross for your sake. Thank him for the free gift of eternal life. Give praise to God the Father for his forgiveness and grace in your life. Give thanks to the Holy Spirit for sealing your salvation for all eternity.

If your answer is *no*, then you can offer to God a prayer of commitment right now. You can invite Jesus to become the Lord of your life right now. If you don't know what to say to Jesus, here is a prayer you can pray:

Dear Lord,

I know that I'm a sinner. I'm sorry for my sin, and I ask you to forgive me. I believe you died for my sins and rose from the dead. I repent of my sins, and I ask you to come into my life and take control. I make a commitment to follow you, and I trust you as my Lord and Savior.

In your name, Amen.

Remember, it's not the words that save you. It's the commitment of your heart that makes you a genuine follower of Jesus. If you prayed that prayer and you mean these words with all your heart, then you have been born again. You'll experience the abundant life in the here and now. And you'll have eternal life in the world to come.

Notes

INTRODUCTION: DOES CHRISTIANITY NEED TO BE SAVED?
1. Jude 1:3

CHAPTER 1: A SHORT HISTORY OF SPIRITUAL DEFECTION
1. Billy Graham, *Just as I Am* (San Francisco: HarperCollins, 1997), 139.
2. Ibid.
3. Will Graham, "The Tree Stump Prayer: When Billy Graham Overcame Doubt," BillyGraham.org, July 9, 2014, https://billygraham.org/story /the-tree-stump-prayer-where-billy-graham-overcame-doubt.
4. Charles Templeton, *Farewell to God: My Reasons for Rejecting the Christian Faith* (Toronto: McClelland & Stewart, 1996), 9.
5. Ibid., 7–8.
6. Lee Strobel, *The Case for Faith* (Grand Rapids: Zondervan, 2000), 13.
7. Ibid., 17–18.
8. Ibid., 18.
9. Genesis 3:1
10. NLT
11. 1 Samuel 3:1
12. 1 Kings 11:1-3
13. Ecclesiastes 7:26
14. 2 Corinthians 6:14
15. See 1 Kings 11:33.
16. 1 Kings 19:10
17. 1 Kings 19:11-12
18. 1 Kings 19:18
19. Jeremiah 2:19
20. See Jeremiah 36 and 38.

21. John 6:2
22. See John 6:5-15.
23. John 6:26-27, 35-36
24. John 6:54-56
25. John 6:60
26. John 6:66
27. John 6:68-69
28. Richard Dawkins, *The God Delusion* (New York: Houghton Mifflin, 2008), 283.
29. John 3:13; 6:38; 8:23
30. John 8:29; 10:36; 16:28
31. John 8:58; 17:24
32. Matthew 20:28; John 3:16-17; 10:9; 14:6
33. Luke 24:25-27; John 5:39
34. John 11:25
35. Matthew 1:20; Luke 1:35
36. Mark 1:9-11
37. Isaiah 7:14; Matthew 1:22-23
38. See Mark 14:61-62; compare with Daniel 7:13-14.
39. John 8:46
40. Matthew 4:23; Mark 4:39; Luke 4:35; John 11:44
41. John 2:19-21; 5:21-22; 10:18
42. Matthew 9:2; Mark 2:1-12; Luke 5:20; 7:48
43. Matthew 16:16-17
44. John 5:18. See also John 10:30-35; Mark 14:64-65.
45. John 8:58; compare with Exodus 3:14.
46. C. S. Lewis, *Mere Christianity* (New York: HarperCollins, 2001), 68.
47. John 8:31-32
48. John 6:38-39, italics added.
49. Ephesians 1:5
50. Romans 8:30
51. 2 Peter 1:10
52. Jude 1:17-19
53. Jude 1:20
54. Hebrews 6:4-6
55. Jude 1:22-23
56. Jude 1:24-25

CHAPTER 2: DESTROYING CHRISTIANITY BY "SAVING" IT

1. Sarah Pulliam Bailey, "Rachel Held Evans, Progressive Christian Author Who Challenged Evangelicals, Dies at 37," *Washington Post*, May 4, 2019,

https://www.washingtonpost.com/religion/2019/05/04/rachel-held-evans
-progressive-christian-author-who-challenged-evangelicals-dies/.

2. Rachel Held Evans, *A Year of Biblical Womanhood: How a Liberated Woman Found Herself Sitting on Her Roof, Covering Her Head, and Calling Her Husband "Master"* (Nashville: Nelson, 2012), 48.

3. Genesis 2:23

4. Evans, *A Year of Biblical Womanhood*, 294.

5. See 2 Timothy 3:16 and 2 Peter 1:21.

6. Evans, *A Year of Biblical Womanhood*, 296. Italics in the original.

7. Robert Moats Miller, *Harry Emerson Fosdick: Preacher, Pastor, Prophet* (New York: Oxford University Press, 1985), 335.

8. This profile of Harry Emerson Fosdick has been adapted from "Harry Emerson Fosdick" in *131 Christians Everyone Should Know*, Mark Galli and Ted Olsen, eds. (Nashville: Broadman & Holman, 2000), 104–106.

9. Hilary Wakeman, *Saving Christianity: New Thinking for Old Beliefs* (Dublin: Liffey Press, 2003), n.p.

10. Ibid.

11. Ibid.

12. Ibid.

13. Ibid.

14. Rachel Held Evans, "Why Millennials Are Leaving the Church," *CNN Belief Blog*, July 27, 2013, http://religion.blogs.cnn.com/2013 /07/27/why-millennials-are-leaving-the-church.

15. Rachel Held Evans, *Evolving in Monkey Town: How a Girl Who Knew All the Answers Learned to Ask the Questions* (Grand Rapids: Zondervan, 2010), 17–18.

16. Rachel Held Evans, *Searching for Sunday: Loving, Leaving, and Finding the Church* (Nashville: Nelson, 2015), 15.

17. Brian McLaren, "The Equation of Change," *On Being* with Krista Tippett, OnBeing.org, March 13, 2014, https://onbeing.org/programs /brian-mclaren-the-equation-of-change.

18. Brian McLaren, *A New Kind of Christianity: Ten Questions That Are Transforming the Faith* (New York: HarperOne, 2010), 138.

19. Dan Barker, *Godless: How an Evangelical Preacher Became One of America's Leading Atheists* (Berkeley, CA: Ulysses Press, 2008), 33–35.

20. Michael Shermer, *How We Believe: The Search for God in an Age of Science*, second edition (New York: Henry Holt, 2000), 2.

21. Ibid., 4.

22. Ibid., 4–5.

23. Ibid., 6–7.

24. John 8:31-32

25. McLaren, *A New Kind of Christianity*, 137–138.
26. Brian McLaren, "Brian McLaren on the Kingdom of God," Pomomusings.com, January 14, 2008; http://pomomusings.com/2008/01/14/brian-mclaren-on-the-kingdom-of-god.
27. Ibid.
28. Ibid.
29. Ibid.
30. Ibid.
31. Matthew 19:29
32. Mark 10:29-30
33. John 3:16
34. John 6:40
35. John 10:28
36. John 17:2
37. Luke 23:43
38. Brian McLaren, "A Tale of Two Gospels," Slideshare.net, slide 9, September 18, 2009, www.slideshare.net/brianmclaren/leading-in-tradition-2017091.
39. Ibid., slide 43.
40. Ibid., slide 44.
41. Galatians 1:6-8
42. Acts 4:12

CHAPTER 3: THE EXTINCTION OF TRUTH

1. Thomas Gray, "Ode on a Distant Prospect of Eton College," Thomas Gray Archive, www.thomasgray.org/cgi-bin/display.cgi?text=odec.
2. Roff Smith, "DNA in London Grave May Help Solve Mysteries of the Great Plague," NationalGeographic.com, September 8, 2016, https://news.nationalgeographic.com /2016/09/bubonic-plague-dna-found-london-black-death.
3. James Leasor, *The Plague and the Fire* (Cornwall, UK: Stratus, 2001), 17–18.
4. Ben Johnson, "The Great Plague 1665—The Black Death," Historic UK, https://www.historic-uk.com/HistoryUK/HistoryofEngland/The-Great-Plague/.
5. Ibid.
6. Leonardo da Vinci, ed. Jean Paul Richter, *The Notebooks of Leonardo Da Vinci*, vol. 2 (Mineola, NY: Dover, 1970), Entry 1168, 292–93.
7. Ibid.
8. The Declaration of Independence, July 4, 1776, http://www.ushistory.org/declaration/document/.

9. Henry Ward Beecher, *Prayers from Plymouth Pulpit* (New York: Charles Scribner, 1867), 8.

10. Amy B. Wang, "'Post-Truth' Named 2016 Word of the Year by Oxford Dictionaries," *Washington Post*, November 16, 2016, www.washingtonpost .com/news/the-fix/wp/2016/11/16/post-truth-named-2016-word-of-the -year-by-oxford-dictionaries/.

11. George Orwell, *Nineteen Eighty-Four* (New York: Knopf, 1992), 6.

12. Marcus J. Borg, *Convictions: How I Learned What Matters Most* (New York: HarperCollins, 2014), 36.

13. Ibid., 38.

14. Marcus J. Borg, *Days of Awe and Wonder: How to Be a Christian in the Twenty-First Century* (New York: HarperCollins, 2017), 27–30.

15. Marcus J. Borg, *The God We Never Knew: Beyond Dogmatic Religion to a More Authentic Contemporary Faith* (New York: HarperCollins, 1997), 25.

16. Ibid.

17. Marcus J. Borg, "Continuing the Resurrection Conversation," Patheos, October 9, 2013, www.patheos.com/blogs/marcusborg/2013/10 /continuing-the-resurrection-conversation.

18. "Jesus Seminar Phase 1: Sayings of Jesus," https://www.westarinstitute.org /projects/the-jesus-seminar/jesus-seminar-phase-1-sayings-of-jesus/.

19. 2 Corinthians 11:13-15

20. See Matthew 5:13-16.

21. John 18:37

22. John 18:38

23. Brian D. McLaren, *A New Kind of Christian: A Tale of Two Friends on a Spiritual Journey* (Minneapolis: Fortress, 2019), xviii. Italics in the original.

24. G. K. Chesterton, *Orthodoxy* (New York: Image, 2014), 27.

25. Brian D. McLaren, *A Generous Orthodoxy: Why I Am a Missional, Evangelical, Post/Protestant, Liberal/Conservative, Mystical/Poetic, Biblical, Charismatic/Contemplative, Fundamentalist/Calvinist, Anabaptist/Anglican, Methodist, Catholic, Green, Incarnational, Depressed-Yet-Hopeful, Emergent, Unfinished Christian* (Grand Rapids: Zondervan, 2004), 170–171.

26. Ephesians 6:14-15

27. Rachel Held Evans, *Evolving in Monkey Town: How a Girl Who Knew All the Answers Learned to Ask the Questions* (Grand Rapids: Zondervan, 2010), 195.

28. Matthew 7:13-14

29. Matthew 22:31; Mark 11:17; 12:26; John 10:34

30. Martyn Lloyd-Jones, *The Cross: God's Way of Salvation* (Wheaton, IL: Crossway, 1986), 144.

31. Brian McLaren, "More on the Emergent Conversation," BrianMcLaren
    .net, November 17, 2014, https://brianmclaren.net/more-on-the
    -emergent-conversation.
32. Ibid.
33. Ibid.

CHAPTER 4: THE POST-TRUTH CHURCH IN A POST-CHRISTIAN WORLD

1. Jude 1:3
2. Matt Kennedy, "July 20, 2017 Show with Matt Kennedy on 'The Liberal
   Episcopalian War against Biblical Anglicans (& How a Historic 19th
   Century Anglican Church Became a Mosque),'" *Iron Sharpens Iron* radio
   podcast, July 21, 2017, www.ironsharpensironradio.com/podcast/july
   -20-2017-show-with-matt-kennedy-on-the-liberal-episcopalian-war
   -against-biblical-anglicans-how-a-historic-19th-century-anglican-church
   -became-a-mosque. Audio transcribed by the author. Quoted section runs
   from 35:25–36:13.
3. Ibid., 36:31–36:51.
4. Ibid., 39:38–39:53.
5. Ibid., 39:54–40:08.
6. Ibid., 40:20.
7. Ibid., 41:17.
8. Ibid., 45:36–45:47. Some details of this story are from Mary Ann
   Mueller, "Binghamton, NY: Episcopal Diocese Sells Historic Church
   to Muslims," VirtueOnline, April 1, 2010; www.virtueonline.org
   /binghamton-ny-episcopal-diocese-sells-historic-church-muslims.
9. Tony Jones, "In Praise of Relativism," Patheos, August 6, 2011, www
   .patheos.com/blogs/tonyjones/2011/08/06/in-praise-of-relativism/.
10. Tony Jones, "What's a Christian to Do with . . . Dan Savage?," Patheos,
    July 11, 2011, www.patheos.com/blogs/tonyjones/2011/07/11/whats
    -a-christian-to-do-with-dan-savage.
11. Ibid.
12. Matthew 5:28
13. Genesis 2:24
14. Hebrews 13:4
15. Jones, "What's a Christian to Do with . . . Dan Savage?"
16. Ibid.
17. 1 Corinthians 5:13
18. 1 Corinthians 5:5
19. Deuteronomy 4:2
20. "The Think Piece Interview: John Shelby Spong," TP Interviews,

October 14, 2013, www.thinkpiecepublishing.com/interviews/the -think-piece-interview-bishop-john-shelby-spong.

21. Richard Dawkins, *The God Delusion* (Boston: Houghton Mifflin, 2006), 269.
22. Brandon Withrow, "They Have Faith Their Church Will Change," Daily Beast, September 25, 2016; www.thedailybeast.com /they-have-faith -their-church-will-change.
23. Ibid.
24. John 8:31-32
25. Andy Crouch, "The Emergent Mystique," *Christianity Today*, November 1, 2004, www.christianitytoday.com/ct/2004/november/12.36.html.
26. Ibid.
27. Ibid.
28. Matthew 7:15-17
29. Jude 1:4
30. Jude 1:3

CHAPTER 5: HOW BIBLICAL TRUTH HAS SHAPED HISTORY

1. Brian D. McLaren, *Everything Must Change: Jesus, Global Crises, and a Revolution of Hope* (Nashville: Thomas Nelson, 2007), 33.
2. Ibid.
3. Ibid., 36.
4. *Hitler's Table Talk, 1941–1945: His Private Conversations*, trans. Norman Cameron and R. H. Stevens, ed. H. R. Trevor-Roper (New York: Enigma Books, 2000–2008), 110.
5. Ibid., 110, 112.
6. *The Goebbels Diaries 1939–1941*, trans. and ed. Fred Taylor (London: Hamish Hamilton, 1982), 77.
7. Alan Bullock, *Hitler: A Study in Tyranny* (New York: HarperPerennial, 1991), 219.
8. Wolfgang Weidlich, *Sociodynamics: A Systematic Approach to Mathematical Modelling in the Social Sciences* (Mineola, NY: Dover Publications, 2006), 159.
9. McLaren, *Everything Must Change*, 33.
10. Robert Louis Wilken, *The First Thousand Years: A Global History of Christianity* (New Haven, CT: Yale University Press, 2012), 307–308.
11. Ephesians 6:5-8
12. Ephesians 6:9
13. Moses I. Finley, *Ancient Slavery and Modern Ideology*, ed. Brent D. Shaw (Princeton, NJ: Markus Wiener, 1998), 11–17; Yvon Garlan, *Slavery in Ancient Greece* (Ithaca, NY: Cornell University Press, 1988), 97.

14. Exodus 21:2
15. Luke 6:31. See also Matthew 7:12.
16. Galatians 3:28
17. 1 Timothy 1:9-10
18. Malachi 2:16
19. Matthew 19:8
20. 2 Corinthians 3:17
21. Revelation 7:9
22. Brian McLaren, *A Generous Orthodoxy* (Grand Rapids, MI: Zondervan, 2004), 35.
23. John 14:6
24. James 4:4
25. 1 Peter 5:8-9
26. See the English Standard Version translation of Matthew 3:2; 4:17; 10:7; and Mark 1:15.
27. Brian McLaren, "A Tale of Two Gospels," Slideshare.net, slide 9, September 18, 2009, www.slideshare.net/brianmclaren /leading-in-tradition-2017091.
28. McLaren, *A Generous Orthodoxy*, 99.
29. Ibid.
30. John 18:36
31. Rachel Held Evans, "The Apologetics Movement Created a Monster," RachelHeldEvans.com, April 5, 2011, https://rachelheldevans.com /blog/apologetics-movement-monster.
32. Jim Wallis, "10 Resolutions for 2015," *Huffington Post*, December 31, 2014, www.huffpost.com/entry/10-resolutions-for-2015_b_6401396.
33. Brian D. McLaren, *A Generous Orthodoxy*, 237.
34. Genesis 2:15, italics added.
35. United Nations Sustainable Development Goals Knowledge Platform, "Transforming Our World: The 2030 Agenda for Sustainable Development," United Nations website, https://sustainabledevelopment .un.org/post2015/transformingourworld.
36. Larry Bell, "The UN's Global Warming War on Capitalism: An Important History Lesson," *Forbes*, January 22, 2013, www.forbes.com/sites/larrybell /2013/01/22/the-u-n-s-global-warming-war-on-capitalism-an-important -history-lesson-2.
37. Ibid.
38. Matthew 25:34-36, 40
39. Luke 14:12-14
40. Luke 10:25-37
41. Jeff Cox, "That $22 Trillion National Debt Number Is Huge, But Here's

What It Really Means," CNBC.com, February 13, 2019, www.cnbc
.com/2019/02/13/that-22-trillion-national-debt-number-is-huge-but
-heres-what-it-really-means.html.

42. David Perdue, "Greatest Threat to Global Security Is America's National
Debt," *The Post and Courier*, June 26, 2018, www.postandcourier.com
/opinion/commentary/greatest-threat-to-global-security-is-america-s
-national-debt/article_f69fb3dc-7975-11e8-823a-a3106cd25b98.html.

43. Matthew 10:42

44. John 4:14

CHAPTER 6: I BELIEVE IN GOD THE FATHER

1. Jude 1:3

2. R. Albert Mohler Jr., *The Apostles' Creed: Discovering Authentic Christianity
in an Age of Counterfeits* (Nashville: Nelson, 2019), xvii.

3. Isaiah 66:13

4. Psalm 139:14

5. Genesis 2:17

6. Genesis 3:1, 4-5

7. Revelation 22:1-3

8. Genesis 2:23-24

9. Revelation 19:7-9

10. Genesis 2:15

CHAPTER 7: I BELIEVE IN JESUS THE SON

1. "Oprah Winfrey Interviews Betty Eadie (Part 1 of 2)," interview on the
Oprah Winfrey Show, March 4, 1993, YouTube, www.youtube.com
/watch?v=6uUiYFaawTU, 14:57–15:38. Transcribed by the author.

2. Acts 4:12

3. John 3:7

4. John 5:37

5. Matthew 3:16-17

6. Mark 9:2-8

7. John 1:32-34

8. John 5:33

9. John 5:31-32

10. John 5:36

11. John 10:30

12. John 10:33

13. Isaiah 9:6; 40:3; 42:1-4; 53:2-10

14. John 5:39-40

15. John 5:41

16. John 6:68
17. John 21:24
18. Genesis 3:15
19. Luke 1:34
20. Luke 1:35
21. 1 Peter 1:19
22. Wayne Grudem, *Systematic Theology: An Introduction to Biblical Doctrine* (Grand Rapids: Zondervan, 2000), 530.
23. John 18:33-38
24. John 14:6
25. John 18:38
26. Hebrews 4:15
27. J. Gresham Machen, "Christianity vs. Modern Liberalism," *Moody Bible Institute Monthly* XXIII, no. 8, April 1923, 352, https://archive.org/details /moodybibleinstit2319mood/page/352.
28. Ibid.
29. Ephesians 4:7-10
30. Paul Davies, "Taking Science on Faith," *New York Times*, November 24, 2007, www.nytimes.com/2007/11/24/opinion/24davies.html.
31. 2 Timothy 2:8
32. 1 Corinthians 15:14-19
33. 1 Corinthians 15:3-4, italics added.
34. Acts 2:29-32, italics added.
35. Hebrews 1:3
36. Acts 2:33-36
37. John 14:2-3
38. Brian McLaren, "A Tale of Two Gospels," Slideshare.net, slide 9, September 18, 2009, www.slideshare.net/brianmclaren /leading-in -tradition-2017091.
39. C. S. Lewis, *Mere Christianity* (New York: HarperCollins, 2001), 134.

CHAPTER 8: I BELIEVE IN THE HOLY SPIRIT

1. 1 Corinthians 12:13
2. John 14:16
3. John 16:13
4. Acts 1:8
5. Ephesians 1:13-14
6. John 6:44
7. "William Bramwell Booth, 1829–1912, His Life and Ministry, A Very Short Biography," Gospel Truth Ministries, www.gospeltruth.net/booth /boothbioshort.htm.

8. Ephesians 4:7-8, 11-13
9. John 15:5

CHAPTER 9: LIVING OUT AN UNCOMPROMISED FAITH

1. Adrian Rogers, keynote address at the 53rd annual National Religious Broadcasters Convention, Indianapolis, Indiana, February 1996.
2. John 17:20-23
3. See John 6:25-66; cf. Exodus 16:4; Nehemiah 9:15; Psalm 78:24-25.
4. John 6:60
5. John 6:66
6. John 6:64
7. John 6:65
8. John 5:39
9. Daniel 9:25
10. Frederick A. Larson, "Daniel's Prophecy," The Star of Bethlehem website, www.bethlehemstar.com/the-day-of-the-cross/daniels-prophecy.
11. Sir Isaac Newton's Observations on the Prophecies of Daniel and the Apocalypse of St. John, quoted in *An Introduction to the Critical Study and Knowledge of the Holy Scriptures, Vol IV*, ed. Thomas Hartwell Horne (London: Longmans, Green, and Co., 1877), 632.
12. James 3:1
13. Numbers 13:31-32
14. Numbers 14:7-9
15. Jeremiah 9:1
16. See Jeremiah 38.
17. 1 Corinthians 14:8
18. John 1:14
19. John 8:11
20. Ibid.
21. 1 Corinthians 6:9

EPILOGUE: "THAT BORN AGAIN THING"

1. Shane Claiborne, *The Irresistible Revolution: Living as an Ordinary Radical* (Grand Rapids: Zondervan, 2016), 86–87.
2. Matthew 4:19
3. Rob Bell, "Love Wins: A Book Excerpt," Patheos, March 16, 2011, www.patheos.com/resources/additional-resources/2011/03/love-wins-a-book-excerpt-rob-bell-03-16-2011.aspx.

About the Author

MICHAEL YOUSSEF is the founder and president of Leading The Way with Dr. Michael Youssef, a worldwide ministry that leads the way for people living in spiritual darkness to discover the light of Christ through the creative use of media and on-the-ground ministry teams (www.LTW.org). His weekly television programs and daily radio programs are broadcast in twenty-five languages and seen worldwide, airing more than thirteen thousand times per week. He is also the founding pastor of The Church of The Apostles in Atlanta, Georgia.

Dr. Youssef was born in Egypt, but in 1984, he fulfilled a childhood dream of becoming an American citizen. He holds numerous degrees, including a PhD in social anthropology from Emory University. He has authored more than thirty-five books, including recent popular titles *The Barbarians Are Here* and *Jesus, Jihad and Peace*. He and his wife have four grown children and several grandchildren.

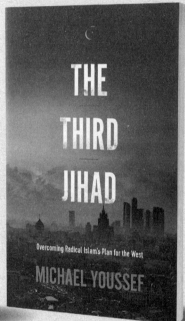